AMERICA
the
VIRTUOUS

AMERICA
the
VIRTUOUS

The Crisis of Democracy
and the Quest for Empire

Claes G. Ryn

Transaction Publishers
New Brunswick (U.S.A.) and London (U.K.)

Library of Congress Catalog Number: 2003055565
ISBN: 0-7658-0219-8
Printed in the United States of America

Library of Congress Cataloging-in-Publication Data

Ryn, Claes G., 1943-
    America the virtuous : the crisis of democracy and the quest for empire / Claes G. Ryn.
        p. cm.
    Includes bibliographical references and index.
    ISBN 0-7658-0219-8 (alk. paper)
    1. United States—Foreign relations—2001- 2. United States—Foreign relations—Philosophy. 3. Democracy—United States. 4. Imperialism. 5. Intervention (International law) 6. Capitalism—Political aspects. 7. Ideology—United States. I. Title.

E895.R96 2003
325'.32'0973090511—dc22   2003055565

*To my daughters Charlotte, Viveka, and Elisabet,
whose world this will be.*

Contents

Acknowledgements

Of the persons who assisted or encouraged my work on this book in some way I should like to mention at least a few. I have discussed the issues explored in these pages for many years with Joseph Baldacchino, the president of the National Humanities Institute, who is as worried as I am about the future of the United States and the Western world. He commented perceptively on parts of the manuscript at various times. Joe also responded with great kindness and patience to pleas for technical assistance from an author who lacks his computer savvy. Thomas D'Evelyn, experienced editor and literary agent, affected the book by properly suggesting that I should lose no time alerting the reader to the large and direct practical political significance of the book's historical and philosophical explorations and that I should not let the reader forget these connections. He gave other advice on structure and saved me from giving some unintended impressions. Jan Olof Bengtsson, a philosophical compatriot with whom I have some friendly disagreements, read the manuscript while finishing his doctoral dissertation at Oxford University. Good questions he raised caused me to clarify, qualify or reinforce some important points. Phillip Henderson, one of my colleagues at the Catholic University of America, who is a keen student of American politics and the presidency, gave me very useful tips about relevant material. David Eisenhower took a keen interest in a part of the manuscript that deals with foreign policy and made astute suggestions. I much appreciate the intellectual generosity of Irving Louis Horowitz, the spirit behind Transaction Publishers. American academic publishing would do well to emulate his openness and tolerance. I am grateful to Laurence Mintz at Transaction for his professionalism and courtesy. Laurence Reardon, one of my doctoral students, gave me helpful reactions when I wondered how what I had written might be perceived. He also prepared the index and provided other assistance.

William F. Byrne was completing his doctoral dissertation under my direction when I finished this book. He knew what I was trying to say and showed me an old framed diploma from his attic that had belonged to his grandfather, a veteran of World War I. The diploma exemplifies the self-righteous nationalism that is discussed in these pages and serves as the frontispiece for the book. Finally, I want to thank my wife, Marianne, who not only read and commented on an early draft of the manuscript, but who, in spite of her own heavy professional responsibilities, keeps picking up the slack in our home that is created by my scholarly endeavors.

An article titled "The Ideology of American Empire," which was adapted from a chapter of this book, appeared in *Orbis. A Journal of World Affairs*, vol. 47, no. 3 (Summer 2003). The publisher of that journal, the Foreign Policy Research Institute in Philadelphia, holds the copyright to the article.

Preface

Over a decade ago, I published a small monograph called *The New Jacobinism*. Considering that it was brought out by the National Humanities Institute rather than a major publisher, it attracted a surprising amount of attention. It received very laudatory reviews. The terms "Jacobinism" and "Jacobins" as labels for certain current phenomena caught on. Demand for the book remained steady. When the fairly substantial press run was nearly exhausted, the question of whether to reprint the book or publish a new edition had to be faced. When I finally concentrated on that question I quickly realized that the original text was a mere sketch, the bare essentials, of an analysis of a large, expanding, and increasingly important subject. I wanted to say a great deal more about the crisis of Western civilization and what is causing it. I saw the need for a more detailed and comprehensive examination of the meaning and import of the new Jacobinism and of how it relates to the cultural, social, and political environment in which it has acquired great influence. I wanted to explain more fully how this expanding ideological and political movement both feeds upon and contributes to the troubles of Western civilization. As I began this work I soon realized that it was taking on a life of its own: I was not merely revising and supplementing the old study; I was writing a new book. In parts of the present volume it is still possible to recognize the old monograph, but that short text has here been thoroughly revised, in effect rewritten, and incorporated into a much larger whole. The title of this book, besides indicating the scope and emphasis of what is offered to the reader, confirms that this is not a new edition of the earlier work.

I wrote the old study with a sense of foreboding regarding the future of the United States and the Western world. In the years since then my worries have only intensified.

Author's Note

At the beginning of each of the following chapters an epigraph consisting of one or more quotations will point to issues to be discussed. Each will have some connection, more or less direct, to the ideology of virtuous empire and democratism. The quotations will not necessarily be from weighty commentators. They may simply give apt and concise expression to a particular notion.

Prologue

War without End

"When we Americans speak seriously about politics, we mean that our principles of freedom and equality and the rights based on them are rational and everywhere applicable. World War II was really an educational project undertaken to force those who did not accept these principles to do so."—Allan Bloom[1]

"There is a value system that cannot be compromised, and that is the values we praise. And if the values are good enough for our people, they ought to be good enough for others."—George W. Bush[2]

"Our responsibility to history is already clear: to answer these attacks and rid the world of evil."—George W. Bush[3]

"Either you are with us, or you are with the terrorists."—George W. Bush[4]

The world may be entering upon an era of protracted and intensifying conflict. It is fashionable to blame the danger of war on a "clash of civilizations," but the main reason why wars may indeed break out is not likely to be the general differences between the old civilizations of the world but modern developments within them that are producing arrogance, inflexibility, intolerance, and belligerence. Such attitudes are more and more common within Western society itself, especially in the United States, which, by dint of its military and economic power, can affect international relations more decisively than any other country.

Attitudes of assertiveness and militancy in dealing with other countries have long been spreading among leading American policymakers. This trend has no single origin, but it can be traced in its most general characteristics to major moral and cultural developments within Western society in the last couple of centuries. It also owes greatly to the specific and very diligent efforts of individuals bent on the creation of

1

an American empire. Since the United States was formed there has been a marked change among leading Americans with regard to their self-understanding and general outlook on life and politics. Importantly, the mentioned moral and cultural trends within Western civilization produced and gave prominence to the idea that societies ought to be radically remade and that those who know what needs to be done should dominate others for their benefit. Communism is a particularly stark example of a plan to improve the human condition that placed unlimited power in the hands of a small elite. Simultaneously, the same trends have liberated the will to power from traditional moral restraints. Power sought and exercised for the good of humanity is thought to be by definition virtuous and to need no restrictions. Today the result is a proliferation of militant, sometimes highly provocative but also moralistic political conduct and speech, as witness the uncompromising attitudes of so many leading American politicians and political intellectuals in discussing how to handle opposition to American aims in the world. What is creating arrogance and saber rattling is not adherence to old Western moral and cultural traditions but an unwillingness to heed them.

A casual observer may be struck most by the *lack* of direction of the present evolution of Western civilization and by the confusion and mixed signals that it emits. Some of the ancient traditions of the West still linger, though in much revised and weakened form, but the initiative belongs to currents that define themselves in opposition to traditional civilization. Paradoxes and tensions abound; Western civilization is indeed not moving in any one direction. Yet careful study reveals large, persistent, and pervasive trends that are in general incompatible with traditional beliefs and that are slowly but surely eroding what remains of those beliefs. Some of these trends can be seen to have formed a synergy and to constitute a largely coherent and sustained alternative to the old ways of the West. Such a general development was clearly discernible just before and during the French Revolution of 1789. Using the name of the intellectuals and political activists who revolutionized France, this movement of radical opposition to traditional Western civilization can be called Jacobinism. In one variant or another this type of political doctrine and action has continued to exert much influence. In the twentieth century, different forms of Jacobinism wielded enormous power, which extended far beyond the Western world. In the second half of the twentieth century, a distinctively American form of Jacobinism evolved from the broader current of hostility to the old West. Its power grew steadily. Its ideology spans a broad range of issues, but its representatives have devoted much of their energy to shaping American foreign policy and have done so with considerable success.

It is partly because of the just-described political movement in the dominant country of Western civilization that the world may have to live through an era of uninterrupted war and other conflict. The movement in question has sharpened and extended an earlier American propensity to make the business of the world its own. Though this movement has some strength in Europe, it is far more deeply entrenched in the United States. A personality type has ascended to great influence in that country that is rhetorically dedicated to doing good for the world but is fundamentally motivated by a will to dominate.

According to a great many philosophers, desiring power over others is one of the permanent and most prominent features of human nature. This desire always threatens to break free of restraints upon it and become tyrannical and ruthless. For that reason, it has been a central purpose of civilization to domesticate and moderate it. Greek culture, as represented by the Theban dramas of Sophocles, warned against that most dangerous of all human propensities, *hubris*. The human being who thinks himself one of the gods and acts accordingly will bring great suffering on others before he is finally struck down by *nemesis*. Christianity, similarly, regarded pride as the cardinal sin. Traditional civilization has taught men to rein in their willfulness through moral self-control and intellectual humility and has created various religious, social, and political supports for this effort. It has sought to subordinate the pursuit of power to life's higher purposes. By checking and subduing it, civilization at its best has reduced the incidence of self-indulgence, arrogance, and belligerence. It has made possible human flourishing by mitigating conflict.

In the most powerful and culturally influential nation of the Western world, the signs are now everywhere that the will to dominate is breaking free of such traditional restraints. This is clear, for instance, from politicians who ignore or neutralize constitutional restrictions on their power and acquire ever-greater control over the lives of their fellow citizens. The will to power is the most palpable in foreign affairs. Not content to wield influence domestically, many politicians and intellectuals seriously contemplate the possibility of ruling the entire world. They regard the United States as having special rights and responsibilities by virtue of its unique commitment to universal principles. They are greatly tempted by the military and economic might of the United States and by the uses to which that power could be put. Many persons who have gained access to the highest levels of policy and opinion making literally dream of making the entire world conform to the wishes of American leaders. One representative voice of these forces is the media commentator Charles Krauthammer, who has long wanted the United States to use its might to effect major changes in the world. It should adopt an "unabashed unilateralism" in behalf of American values. "The U.S. can reshape, indeed remake, reality on its own."[5] Americans of an earlier era would have regarded such ambition as incompatible with humility, indeed, as megalomaniacal.

This kind of desire for power rarely shows itself in its own tawdry voraciousness. Those who have it want not only to dominate others but feel good about doing it, even want to have the applause of others for assuming such high responsibility. They feel the need to dress up their striving in appealing garb. Hence the will to power almost always presents itself as benevolent concern for others, as an unselfish wish to improve society or the world. The desire for empire is thus accompanied by a noble-sounding ideology for how to make the world better. So benevolent and comprehensive are its objectives that those charged with carrying them into practice must have virtually unlimited power.

There was a time when a radically different view of the responsibilities of individuals and nations held sway in America. That view was centered on the need to mind your own business. This was regarded as a demanding task, for, man being morally weak and otherwise imperfect, trying to remedy one's own weaknesses and marshal one's own strengths gave one a great deal to do, usually quite enough to consume one's moral energy. This attitude was reflected in thinking about foreign relations when President George Washington warned in his Farewell Address of the dangers of foreign entanglements. Washington represented the outlook on life of most Americans at the time. The primary task of individuals, communities, or people was to make the best of themselves. By doing so they would contribute indirectly to the well-being of others.

But today a very different sense of priorities has gained wide currency. Political virtue is to try to make the best of others. To wish to run other people's lives, for their benefit, is the "right" thing to do. As if by sheer coincidence, this benevolence has the effect of increasing the power of the allegedly virtuous reformer.

Relative to the society of the early Americans, as represented by George Washington and the Framers of the United States Constitution, America has undergone a profound transformation. The change most relevant in the present context is not population growth, geographical expansion, or technological and economic development. The most significant change is one of fundamental beliefs about human nature and society. As will be shown in this book, the predominant self-understanding of Americans is no longer what it used to be. One of the consequences is the widespread appearance and ascent to power of a personality type almost the reverse in regard to moral and political demeanor of that admired by earlier Americans. Politics always involves an element of assertiveness and pursuit of power, but Americans used to idolize persons whose conduct showed not only political skill and courage but self-restraint and humility. They were quick to detect and condemn mere self-seeking. Today people of relentless and transparent personal ambition can gain influence, provided their wish for power comes wrapped in idealistic verbiage. More and more American leaders, political and intellectual, are blatantly arrogant and anxious to expand their own influence.

When the communist movement aspired to world dominance in the name of the good of humanity it was widely and rightly condemned. Communism caused human suffering of unimaginable proportions. But some who opposed communism did so in part because they did not want this competition for world dominance. They thought they had a much better idea for how the world should look. Now that communism has been defeated people of that kind are trying to implement their own plan for global control. The result is a major movement in behalf of American world hegemony, not to say armed supremacy. A large and growing number of theorists and activists are joining the cause.

A conceited view of self is becoming more and more common that animates a quest for political-ideological empire. This view contrasts sharply with the humility and self-limitation of an older American personality, represented most prominently by George Washington. That personality feared not only unbounded political power but human arrogance. When, in 1789, Washington proclaimed a day of thanksgiving for the benefits bestowed by Almighty God on the American people, his affirmation of the appropriateness of gratitude was indistinguishable from his stressing the fallen nature of man. Americans should unite "in most humbly offering our prayers and supplications to the Great Lord and Ruler of nations and beseech Him to pardon our national and other transgressions."[6] Today many point to America being blessed in a spirit of smugness and do so in order to justify its dominating the world. The humility characteristic of the older kind of American is becoming rare in leading political circles. All but gone as well is the old notion, set forth in a 1630 sermon by John Winthrop, governor of the Massachusetts Bay Company, that America should be like a "city on a hill,"[7] try to become a model for other nations and influence them not by force but by example. In a 1996 article in *Foreign Affairs*, perhaps the most prestigious organ of the American foreign policy establishment inside or outside of government, William Kristol and Robert Kagan expressed their disdain for this old notion. Although it reveals a certain smugness of its own, it contains a strong presumption against international meddling, and this is what Kristol and Kagan could not accept. They urged on the United States the very opposite attitude: "A policy of sitting atop a hill and leading by example in practice is a policy of cowardice and dishonor."[8] One notes that, in their view, American interventionism is dictated by the noblest of principles, specifically, honor and courage.

After the attack on the United States on September 11, 2001, the president of the United States abandoned his earlier stated reservations about an activist and interventionist American foreign policy. With surprising speed he moved away from the view of America's role that he had espoused during his election campaign. Urged on by such long-standing, dedicated, and articulate proponents of American empire as Deputy Secretary of Defense Paul Wolfowitz, the president soon came around to the need for American world dominance, a switch of views that put his repeated calls in the election campaign for a more "humble" U.S. foreign policy in a strange light. In a series of speeches and especially in a strategy statement to the U.S. Congress (which will be discussed later in this book) in September of 2002, the president now cited the exceptional and superior character of the United States as justifying its playing a missionary role in the world. The United States could not be satisfied with military strength sufficient to deter attacks upon it and its allies. It had to have such overwhelming might that potential rivals would not dare to contest its will. Declaring yet another major expansion of American power, the president reserved to the United States the right to strike *preemptively* against any possible threat. The strategic plan was even more ambitious. The president claimed for the United States the role of not only keeping the peace but of making the world "better": The foreign policy of the United States should promote American principles in the world. In an interview with *Washington Post* assistant managing editor Bob Woodward, the president asserted that American values are not just for Americans. "These are God-given values. These aren't United States-created values."[9] The implication was clear: To spread American values was to be on the side of God, to resist them was to oppose God. Often in his public statements the president appeared to be under the influence of a triumphalist sectarian Christianity that breaks down the old distinction between religion and politics and identifies American might with the will of God. The president did not shrink from the military requirements of the new American global strategy or from the need to deal with opposition to it. In a taped interview he made the following comment: "We will export death and violence to the four corners of the earth in defense of our great nation."[10]

Lingering traditional attitudes about self and nation made many Americans uneasy about this kind of global ambition, but a justifiable desire to punish the perpetrators of the attack on the United States and to head off further attacks also made them receptive to calls for a far-reaching battle against "evil" in general and terrorism in particular. This inclination boosted the fortunes of the political and intellectual activists who had long argued in favor of the United States launching a campaign for political and military world hegemony. Most Americans did not see action against terrorists and their supporters as part of a design for global control, but those who did took full advantage of the opportunity to commit the United States to a comprehensive plan for empire.

Though most well-educated Americans are only vaguely aware of it, the government of the United States is heavily influenced by an ideology for global reconstruction that assumes America's moral superiority and right to take charge of the needed changes. On what it considers moral grounds, this ideology mandates worldwide adoption of "democracy," "freedom," "equality," and "capitalism." This mandate provides a justification for throwing off traditional restraints on the will to power and for exercising American power on the largest possible scale. People whom the ideology defines as virtuous are entitled to rule the world for its benefit. According to this ideology, the United States is no ordinary nation. It is based on universal principles, the principles of all mankind, and has a higher responsibility and mission than all other countries. The United States is properly humanity's moral and political leader, the arbiter of good and evil in the world. This vision amounts to a new myth of America: the United States as the ruler of a virtuous empire.

George W. Bush has described the world as divided between two starkly opposed forces. The one side, led by the United States, loves what Bush summarizes as "freedom." The other side hates it. In the president's own words, "Either you're with those who love freedom or you're with those who hate innocent life."[11]

As the United States is called to bestow its high principles and general benevolence on all of humanity, it must of course have power over all of humanity. Since communism, no ideology has provided so much stimulation for the will to power, and many of America's leading policymakers are embracing this doctrine.

The ideology of virtuous empire envisions the remaking not only of the world but of America. The United States must become more faithful to its own principles, but as these are defined by the ideology. What is required is a redefinition of the United States as inherited from the American and Western past and as conceived by the Framers of the Constitution. The ideology wants to replace the historically existing America with its own principles, just as it wants to empty out the past of other nations—all of this for the sake of a better world. The representatives of this movement want to dismantle the old America but also use American military and economic might to implement their vision for humanity.

Those desiring empire realize that this cause will require colossal resources. As the United States has more of them than any other country, they are making a concerted attempt to control its destiny. Many obstacles will have to be removed for the vision of a new world to be realized. Among them are societies and cultures that resist the introduction of American principles. Such recalcitrance can be overcome through the military and economic superiority of the United States.

Because the ideology of virtuous empire envisions not only American world dominance but the remaking of the world in its image, it is a recipe for conflict and perpetual war. The moralistic aggressiveness that it inspires is certain to inflame international relations. It is certain to provoke opposition and hostility. Indeed, it has already done so. The ideology is not yet the sole inspiration of American foreign policy, but it has exercised enough influence to create deepening dissonance between the United States and other nations and regions.

It is high time that Americans and others become aware of the nature of this quest for global hegemony. The eleventh hour may be upon us. The forces of virtuous empire are wielding enormous power, and yet the ideology that informs its efforts is only very imperfectly known to those outside the movement, whether they be in politics, the media, the universities, or the general educated public. To the extent that the ideology is known at all, it is in bits and pieces or as an ad hoc rationale for an assertive policy against terrorism. But the militancy in foreign policy forms part of a comprehensive effort to make the world pliable to the designs of a new elite.

The ideology as a whole needs to become widely and fully understood so that the dangers that it poses to the West and the world can also be fully recognized. Without this kind of awareness much of current American politics will be hard to understand, and without it there can be no intelligent, concerted opposition to the push for world dominance.

This book will examine in depth what lies behind the drive for virtuous empire and what are its ultimate objectives. It will show how this drive fits into a more general view of life and politics. The book will explore the transformation of the American mind and character and how it has contributed to the outward quest.

The purpose is to make possible a more well-informed and focused discussion of major trends within today's Western civilization and politics. Fully to explain the meaning and significance of the mentioned ideology, its various components have to be examined in a historical and philosophical perspective and in relation to the great difficulties already facing Western civilization. Much of the book will be taken up with the nature and extent of those problems. Besides showing how these problems relate to the rise of imperialistic ideology, the aim will be to indicate possibilities for defusing moralistic militancy and more generally for reinvigorating a faltering Western society. Examining the ideology of empire serves this larger purpose.

The following study of dangerous trends within Western society, mostly as they appear in its most powerful country, will raise questions about what an alternative to them might look like. Implicit in the book's analysis and critique of imperialistic ideology and other social and political phenomena is the possibility of moving in a different direction. The chapters to follow will not formulate an elaborate, fully fledged alternative to what is scrutinized, but the outlines of a different approach to the large questions involved will become more and more visible as the book moves towards its conclusion.

It will be necessary to proceed with care to explain the full significance of the ideas and phenomena under examination. The mode of discussion may on occasion seem overly philosophical and scholarly. Yet, as should be obvious from this prologue, the book is not an abstract academic exercise of little practical import. The very opposite is the case. Though the issues to be explored will at times require some fairly difficult philosophical explication and analysis, all of them are directly relevant to the great questions of the day, including, most especially, that of war and peace.

Though the evidence has yet to be presented, it should be stated here and now that should the ideology of empire continue to feed and justify the will to power of those who make the most important decisions for the Western world, not only are wars inevitable, but Western civilization, already strained by severe problems, will in time suffer major hardships and social turbulence. Contrary to its rhetoric, the ideology of virtuous empire helps erode what remains of more traditional forms of self-discipline and responsibility. If present trends continue, America and its European allies will, for the fore-seeable future, have to devote much more of their resources and energy to military operations, some of them on a scale that will make incursions of earlier years appear trivial. Under the influence of universalist ideology, the United States will not only encounter growing hostility abroad but create chronic insecurity at home. There are likely to be more ruptures and fissures in the American-European relationship. The United States will have to pursue wars without borders in which traditional military campaigns are not as relevant. It will have to contend first of all with a hostile Muslim world and more generally with intensifying resentment around the world. The United States and its increasingly reluctant allies will have to handle these huge challenges while the moral and cultural foundations of Western civilization continue to crumble. To some, these are merely imaginary risks; to some, they seem an acceptable cost for advancing the global cause of political virtue. This book will question not just the cost but the virtue.

The push for American empire is portrayed by its proponents as a great moral cause. It is not driven by a will to dominate but a wish to serve peace and human well-being. In the history of ancient Rome the period from the Punic Wars to Augustus saw the rise of a similar, more and more blatant desire for empire. Joseph Schumpeter (1883-1950), the economist and social thinker, pointed to that era as "the classic example of that kind of insincerity in both foreign and domestic affairs which permeates not only avowed motives but also probably the conscious motives of the actors themselves—of that policy which pretends to aspire to peace but unerringly generates war, the policy of continual preparation for war, the policy of meddlesome interventionism."[12] It is highly pertinent in the context of this book that Rome's growing appetite for empire is commonly seen as a symptom and source of Rome's decline and fall.

Historians sometimes identify moments in the past that seem to have been major turning points—events and decisions that ended one era and inaugurated another. People living at the time were largely unaware that they stood at a watershed, but their actions, whether unthinking or deliberate, permanently and markedly changed their societies. Western civilization may just now be in the middle of such a momentous epoch, a time when what used to be mere potentialities suddenly acquired new strength, broke out of earlier constraints and overwhelmed the ways and ideas of the older society. The change within American and Western society as a whole ultimately involves a new view of man, society, and the world and has palpable political, moral, cultural, and intellectual manifestations. Western civilization is being redefined and reorganized in the light of approaches to life that are much different from those that gave rise to the same civilization in the first place. Much of that work is pioneered in the United States by persons whose ultimate dream is to preside over American empire. Some of the changes they initiate will prove highly destructive, even suicidal.

Under the influence of questionable elites, the Western world may indeed have passed the point of no return in the progressive destruction of its old traditions. Yet those who live at a particular time never know all the potentialities of the present. It may still be possible on the basis of a realistic assessment of the predicament of Western civilization to make choices that will shore up humility and peacefulness and avert the danger of war without end. It may be possible more generally to strengthen or reconstruct the foundations of Western society. This book is written in that hope.

A heavy burden rests on the shoulders of those who are at present guiding the destiny of the West. Many of the most powerful are Americans. The danger is great that these elites will set the world on a course of perpetual conflict. A conceited desire for power may lead Western society and mankind as a whole to catastrophe. The historians of the future will be greatly interested in how Western statesmen and intellectuals handled this dangerous situation. They will be able to tell whether the peoples of the West headed more or less blindly for disaster or were able, in the nick of time, to avert it.

Notes

1.   Allan Bloom, *The Closing of the American Mind* (New York: Simon and Schuster, 1987), 153.
2.   Remarks by President George W. Bush in taped interview with Bob Woodward, *Washington Post*, November 19, 2002, excerpted from Woodward, *Bush at War* (New York: Simon & Schuster, 2002).
3.   Remarks, National Cathedral, September 14, 2001.
4.   Speech to a joint session of the U.S. Congress, September 20, 2002.
5.   Charles Krauthammer, *Time*, March 5, 2001.
6.   George Washington, Presidential Proclamation of a Day of Thanksgiving, 1789.

7.   John Winthrop, "A Model of Christian Charity," sermon given in 1630; the quoted words taken from Matthew 5:14.

8.   William Kristol and Robert Kagan, "Toward a Neo-Reaganite Foreign Policy," *Foreign Affairs*, July/August, 1996.

9.   Remarks by President George W. Bush in taped interview with Bob Woodward, *Washington Post*, November 19, 2002.

10.   Taped interview quoted in Bob Woodward, *Bush at War*, 352.

11.   George W. Bush, presidential address, Fort Hood, January 3, 2003.

12.   Joseph Schumpeter, *Imperialism and Social Class* (New York: Augustus M. Kelley, 1951), 66.

1

The Crisis of Western Civilization and the Rise of Jacobinism

"There is no intellectual ground remaining for any regime other than democracy."
—*Allan Bloom[1]*

"Liberalism has won and there are no more contenders."—Francis Fukuyama[2]

We live in the age of democracy. People in the Western world take democracy for granted. They see this form of government and life as part of the natural order of things. Western democracy is assumed to be strong, permanent, and invulnerable.

Yet historically and philosophically informed observation and reflection raise grave doubts about Western democracy's ability to survive in the long run. Perhaps the most compelling sign of trouble is the complacency that marks most public discussion of democracy. Many commentators proclaim democracy's triumph over evil political forces in the world and hold up today's Western society as a model for all humanity. They do so in the face of glaring symptoms of social decay. Contrary to widespread belief, evidence is accumulating that Western democracy is in continuous and precipitous decline. The following brief list is merely suggestive: political self-seeking, opportunism, demagoguery and other irresponsibility, erosion of the rule of law, attitudes of self-indulgence and short-sightedness, the disintegration of the family, crime and other dishonesty, declining standards of professional conduct, corporate wrongdoing, drug abuse, sexual promiscuity, academic shoddiness and extremism, religious superficiality and sentimentalism, priestly misconduct, crudity and debauchery in the arts and entertainment, general vulgarization of life. In their pervasiveness these and other phenomena indicate a disintegration of civilization. Among the most compelling and ominous signs of democracy's decline is a growing conformity and a sharpening intolerance of opinions that deviate from those dominating the mass media, the universities, and government. Public debate stays within a narrow and shrinking range, and those who dare to step outside of it risk being ostracized or demonized and losing their careers or livelihood.

Still, the problems of democracy are, if not ignored, widely discounted, evaded, or misunderstood. The complacency about the problems of Western democracy is perhaps never more glaring than when commentators cite a statistic for a particular year which shows, for example, a dip in some forms of crime, a rise in SAT scores, or a falling rate of a venereal disease, as if any of these or a few of them together were evidence that life in general is improving. Some seriously contend that present-day Western society represents the culmination of mankind's historical struggle for enlightenment and well-being, that its ideas and institutions signal "the end of history." Now that Western democracy has been discovered to be superior to all other possible forms of government, so the argument goes, old intellectual conflicts will peter out and backward regimes will disappear, one by one. At a time when the problems of democracy might seem to raise questions about its survival, a new ideology—which in one of its prominent aspects may be called democratism—puts great emphasis on democracy's superiority and missionary task. The late political thinker Allan Bloom, author of the best-selling book *The Closing of the American Mind* (1987), was just one voice in a chorus when he proclaimed, "There is no intellectual ground remaining for any regime other than democracy."[3]

The theme that mankind has finally reached its political destiny is not new. In the 1950s Daniel Bell and other social democrats and liberals predicted the eventual disappearance of all competition to Western-style popular government and the welfare state, so obvious were their superiority to other possible political arrangements. Today this self-praise has acquired a new fervor and become the justification for an assertive foreign policy—as if the superiority of Western democracy were not so self-evident after all but needed to be conveyed to other parts of the world through political pressure and force. Democratism is not yet the sole influence on the formation of American foreign policy, but it exercises great power.

Given the signs of serious trouble in the West, the spread and intensification of this democratist zeal can be seen as symptomatic of a flight from reality or as a cynical exploitation of moods of escape. The democratist self-satisfaction is ubiquitous and often appears frantic. The celebration of democracy hangs like a narcotic cloud over the public, inducing an intellectual daze and spells of euphoria. No realistic assessment of the state of Western democracy is possible without first breathing a great deal of fresh air.

One of the purposes of this book is to identify and analyze what may be democracy's central problem. Before some reflections can be presented regarding its present condition in the West and its likely prospects, it is necessary to take up several closely connected philosophical issues. First of all, two different meanings of the term "democracy" need to be distinguished. One of the symptoms of democracy's precarious state is the uncritical manner in which the word is used. In both theory and practice two radically different notions of popular government are blurred. It will be argued here that only one of these is compatible with liberty and civilized life. At a time when many countries are moving away from totalitarianism and are reaffirming or shaping national identities, the Western democracies, for all of their wealth, conveniences, and technological prowess, are in some respects setting very poor examples. It would not be strange if, in the eyes of discriminating observers around the world, they were discrediting democracy. The assumption that criticism of the United States and the West from other parts of the world must be due solely to envy shows both conceit and lack of imagination.

Although the difficulties of Western democracy are manifold and have no single source, the most important can be traced directly or indirectly to a deficiency at the moral center. The state of democracy is due in large part to the abandonment of an older notion of morality and character and a resulting evasion of individual responsibility. More than any other possible regime democracy needs a population of character. The same ethical considerations that are necessary in defining a civilized form of popular government are important in defining sound nationhood. In the United States, constitutionalism and life in general are suffering the consequences of the virtual disappearance of what used to be called "republican virtue." The concrete and specific personal obligations of the here and now that were central to an older Western morality are being replaced by an allegedly superior concern about more abstract and distant objectives. The new morality involves empathy for large aggregates of people rather than individuals or groups in the vicinity of the bearer. As the imagination comes to concern itself with the needs of impersonal collectives, attention is distracted from the tasks facing the person up close. Individual and concrete responsibilities—what Christianity spoke of as "love of neighbor"—begin to appear insignificant in comparison to great tasks to be performed far away. The burden of moral effort is shifted from individuals, families, small groups, and local communities. As will be explained, the continual expansion and centralization of the modern democratic state both manifest and aggravate an erosion or abdication of personal responsibility. A few basic distinctions and definitions will make it easier to discern the extent and import of the problems of present-day Western democracy. They will also make it possible to recognize the spuriousness of some current efforts to shore up democracy by making it more "virtuous" and more ambitious abroad.

The profound problems of democracy show the effects of moral, cultural, and political tendencies that have long worked their influence in the Western world. Many of the phenomena that today threaten constitutional popular government can be traced back to sentiments and ideas that gained prominence in connection with the French Revolution that began in 1789. A vision of a new egalitarian social and political order and of popular rule freed not only from traditional elites but from traditional moral and cultural restraints of all kinds had been formulated with great imaginative power by Jean-Jacques Rousseau (1712-1778) a few decades earlier. Rousseau's notion of the natural goodness of man gave rise to a radical redefinition of moral virtue and of the preconditions for a good society. His denial of a darker side of human nature—what Christianity sometimes discusses in terms of "original sin"—undermined the ancient belief that checks, internal and external, must be placed on individual and collective action. His idea that man is naturally good formed the basis for his belief that the popular majority of the moment should have unlimited power. Rousseau portrayed existing society as darkly and severely oppressive in all of its aspects, including the arts and the sciences. The latter enslaved man even more powerfully than government. Rousseau wrote of people in existing societies that "the sciences, letters and the arts . . . spread garlands of flowers over the iron chains with which they are burdened." In his most famous political work, the *Social Contract* (1762), Rousseau proclaimed, "Man is born free, and everywhere he is in chains."[4] Overturning traditionally formed civilization and instituting equality and majoritarian popular rule would be the virtuous course.

In France, Rousseau's view of man and his vision of a new society spread quickly and soon became a powerful political force. It was espoused with increasing militancy by the Jacobin clubs, which saw themselves as incorruptible guardians of universal principles. The moral and ideological fervor of the Jacobins played a crucial role before and during the French Revolution. Jacobin societies sprang up in all parts of France. They derived their name from the movement having evolved from a large club that met at a Jacobin convent in Paris. The Paris Jacobins, who had no less than twelve hundred members by 1790, set the standards of rhetoric, agitation and ceremony for the clubs in the provinces, many of which had hundreds of members. The clubs became incubators for theorizing and political activism of a strongly moralistic type. They combined features of a school, a debating society, a political organization, and a church. Their egalitarianism and denunciation of the existing political and social order became increasingly radical. The Jacobins made sharp rhetorical attacks on what were regarded as conspiracies against "the people." The Jacobins saw themselves as virtuous champions of a great moral cause and as joined by fraternity and solidarity. They were guardians of revolutionary principles. They were ushering in a new way of life, a society of equality and democracy, a glorious goal that permitted no mercy for those who stood in the way. Jacobinism inspired the French Revolution's murderous hatred of traditional elites, its reign of terror, and its messianic ambitions.[5]

Maximilien Robespierre (1758-1794) was a leading Jacobin ideologue and orator. He became a central figure in the Revolution and leader of France. For him, France and humanity faced a clear-cut alternative. The choice was between virtue, freedom, and popular rule, which was the cause of the Jacobins, and evil and oppression, which were the essence of the existing order. Robespierre was an ardent admirer of Rousseau. He read him repeatedly and deliberately sought to implement his political and moral ideas. He believed passionately in Rousseau's notion of virtue, and like Rousseau he wanted a complete transformation of society, the removal of all that stood in the way of the triumph of the new virtue. Jacobin politics was for Robespierre the same as morality, an effort to effectuate universal principles.

A feature of Jacobinism that has held great appeal for many later political thinkers and actors is its strong, if unofficial, elitism. Though the Jacobins spoke and acted in the name of the welfare of the people, the Jacobins assumed that they themselves, as the possessors of virtue and deep insight, would have to lead the people in the direction in which it would want to go, if it understood what its leaders understood. The Jacobins here set the precedent for later political movements championing "the people." These movements would be centrally generated and led rather than driven by spontaneous radical sentiment at the grassroots. In today's Western world, too, the rhetoric of democratism conceals that democracy operates increasingly by central direction. For the most part, the people vote as their leaders, supported by allies in the mass media, want them to vote. Less and less does "popular rule" mean that people make decisions for themselves in their families, associations, and local communities where they can exercise direct or fairly direct control over their own lives. More and more, "popular rule" means that they are content to cede such power to leaders and to accept decisions that are made for them at a great distance from their places of life and work.

The Jacobin spirit has had many manifestations, more or less extreme, since the eighteenth century. It has sometimes been balanced and moderated within particular movements by countervailing influences, but under varying names and in different forms the Jacobin spirit has remained strong. It has continued to direct hostility against the old Western civilization, especially its religious and moral assumptions and its violations of the principle of equality. If the Jacobin spirit suffered a major defeat with the collapse of the Soviet Union and the discrediting of communism, it is today also experiencing a resurgence.

Within today's Western democracies a new Jacobinism is exercising growing influence, especially in the United States. It is working to sever the remaining connections between popular government and the traditional Western view of man and society. It employs an idiom somewhat different from that of the earlier Jacobinism, and it incorporates various new ideological and other ingredients, but it is essentially continuous with the old urge to replace historically evolved societies with an order framed according to abstract, allegedly universal principles, notably that of equality. Like the old Jacobinism, it does not oppose economic inequalities, but it scorns traditional religious, moral, and cultural preconceptions and social patterns that restrict or channel social and political advancement and economic activity—a subject that will be explored in depth in later chapters. The new Jacobins are more accepting of existing society than were the old Jacobins, for they regard today's Western democracy as the result of great moral, social and political progress since the eighteenth century. They see it as an approximation of what universal principles require.

The old Jacobins assumed that their principles were for all peoples, but as they faced pressing and specific obstacles near to home and were culturally focused on France and Europe they did not, for the most part, think globally. The new Jacobins do. They put great stress on the international implications of their principles. The new Jacobinism is indistinguishable from democratism, the belief that democracy is the ultimate form of government and should be installed in all the societies of the world. The new Jacobinism is the main ideological and political force behind present efforts to turn democracy into a worldwide moral crusade.

Not only do the new Jacobins advocate spreading democracy to distant places, but they claim to have the remedy for such problems as the Western democracies still have. What precisely the new Jacobins have in mind for Western society and the world will be discussed at length in this book.

A sign of the power of the new Jacobinism is that it is well represented across the political-intellectual spectrum. It is common among liberals and socialists, many of whom consciously trace their own ideological lineage to the French Revolution. Paradoxically, in the United States the new Jacobinism also finds expression among people called "conservatives" or "neoconservatives." This is a curious fact considering that modern, self-conscious conservatism originated in opposition to the ideas of the French Revolution. The person commonly regarded as the father of modern conservatism, the British statesman and thinker Edmund Burke (1729-97) focused his scorching critique of the French Revolution precisely on Jacobin thinking.

As ever more extreme ideas emanate from today's leading universities and cultural institutions and are transmitted to people in general through the mass media and popular culture, notions that were considered radical some decades earlier begin to look rather staid and old fashioned, and those who defend them begin to seem "conservative." Yet by historical standards the ideas that these persons want to conserve are actually radical in the sense that they are hard to reconcile with the old Western view of man and society. Even the radicalism of the French Jacobins starts to appear conservative when compared to the most extreme forms of radicalism, for example, of the frankly and ruthlessly totalitarian variety.

Powerful historical trends are helped along by the opportunism of people who care more deeply about having the approval of the powers-that-be and about advancement in their careers than about their own deepest convictions. Today the spread of radical attitudes in academia, publishing, journalism, religion, the arts, and elsewhere make many people with a lingering attachment to the old Western tradition shrink from affirming it in ways that may be blatantly offensive to those who set the tone in those fields. Really to challenge the moral, intellectual, and cultural powers in the ascendant is to jeopardize one's standing in society and risk losing the rewards that come from being in tune with the times and pandering to the arbiters of acceptable opinion. To the extent that the old but disapproved beliefs are not hidden or given up, means are found by opportunists holding them to present them in ways more pleasing to the zeitgeist or at least more pleasing to its least extreme representatives. The old beliefs undergo a subtle change. They are discovered by their bearer to be not quite so distant from the favored opinions of the day as once thought. Fear and opportunism work to the same end of transforming old beliefs.

Many cooperate in this partly self-deluding work of attunement to the new order. The new Jacobins enjoy considerable acceptance in the media, indeed, can be said to be a part of the media elite. For that reason, many conservatives who feel stymied by an inhospitable media and university culture hope to gain favor with the powers-that-be by mimicking the new Jacobins. The latter facilitate this rapprochement by claiming to be defenders of Western civilization against the left, which sounds reassuring to the conservatives. Though many of the new Jacobins are quite conscious of and deliberate in the pursuit of their own ideological and political objectives, opportunistic and intellectually less than sophisticated conservatives do not notice that what the new Jacobins defend as Western civilization is actually but a small and relatively recent part of it, chiefly that part which came to political prominence with the French Revolution and that finds its other beginnings in the rationalism of the eighteenth-century Enlightenment and its precursors. To the extent that the new Jacobins do not reject the older Western civilization completely, they radically reinterpret it, as when putative defenders of Christianity find it to be the religion of democracy or when putative defenders of classical political thought find Plato to be a democrat in disguise. Such "traditionalists" can expect more friendly treatment in the media and the universities than traditionalists who find much to defend in the older Christian and classical civilization. The desire for approval and credibility serves the powers-that-be well. It is one of the many factors making it possible for the zeitgeist to co-opt what it does not openly attack.

The new Jacobinism is in important respects different from the kind of radicalism that is today associated with so-called "postmodernism." The latter rejects the notion of "universal principles," and the new Jacobins attack what they regard as the moral nihilism of postmodernism. What the two movements have in common in spite of major disagreements is a desire to destroy the spiritual, cultural, and intellectual inheritance that was challenged by the Enlightenment and the French Revolution. What the new Jacobins defend as Western civilization is the *enlightened,* "modern" West. They see their own allegedly universal principles, such as "democracy," "equality," and "freedom," as derived from Enlightenment thinking. In a widely misinterpreted book, Allan Bloom complained about "the closing of the American mind." As will be demonstrated later, the mind whose closing Bloom bemoaned was the Enlightenment mind. It was this mind, he asserted, that founded America. Though prepared to jettison the older Western civilization, the new Jacobins seem to the postmodernists insufficiently radical—"conservative" even—in that they embrace the rationalism and general ideology of the Enlightenment and the French Revolution, which means to the postmodernists that they are attempting to uphold another oppressive intellectual and political regime.

As understood in this book, the new Jacobinism is not a movement with settled boundaries, definite membership or precise, generally agreed-upon ideological definition. No single contemporary source provides a standard of orthodoxy. A number of writers contribute to the evolution of the ideology and vie for intellectual primacy. The new Jacobinism manifests itself in many fields, but its main interest is politics and political theory. It influences people in varying ways and in varying degrees. Often it is blended in particular persons with ideas and personality traits of very different origin. One of the reasons why the new Jacobinism needs to be differentiated is that it is so frequently in conflict with other, more salutary beliefs held by the same person and stand in the way of the fuller development of those beliefs. Yet the new Jacobinism has its own discernible moral-intellectual momentum and direction and rhetorical tenor. The name here chosen to describe it points to its striking resemblance to an older form of missionary zeal, one that profoundly changed the Western world and permanently affected mankind as a whole. More than any other figure of the past, Rousseau may embody the moral, imaginative, and intellectual stance in which the Jacobin spirit finds its purest expression.

Notes

1.   Bloom, *Closing*, 330.
2.   Francis Fukuyama, "The End of History," *National Interest*, 16 (summer 1989).
3.   Bloom, *Closing*., 330.
4.   Jean-Jacques Rousseau, *The Basic Political Writings* (Indianapolis, IN: Hackett Publishing Co., 1987), *First Discourse*, 3 and *Social Contract*, bk. I, ch. I, 141.
5.   On the French Jacobins, see Simon Schama, *Citizens* (New York: Alfred A. Knopf, 1989), a detailed and richly evocative chronicle of the French Revolution, and Michael Kennedy, *The Jacobin Clubs in the French Revolution* (Princeton, NJ: Princeton University Press, 1982).

2

The New Jacobinism

"What is missing from today's conservatism is the appeal to American greatness . . . . American nationalism . . . is that of an exceptional nation founded on a universal principle."—William Kristol and David Brooks[1]

Neo-Jacobin ideology will be described and analyzed in considerable detail in this book. A brief preliminary sketch beyond what has already been said will help orient the reader to its general characteristics. Perhaps the most fundamental idea of the new Jacobinism is that the United States is an exceptional nation that was founded on universal principles and that all of mankind, heeding the American example, should adopt a single model of social and political life. That model is most commonly summarized in the term "democracy," but the new Jacobins see a close connection between what they call democracy and what they call capitalism. As they understand the latter, it is, like democracy, a progressive force. As will be shown at length below, one of the main reasons why the new Jacobins like capitalism is that they regard it as a powerful agent for remaking traditional societies. Needless to say, not all intellectuals and politicians who are favorable to democracy or capitalism are ipso facto new Jacobins. Both of the mentioned terms can mean very different things. A person may defend popular rule and still recognize that no one form of government is appropriate to all peoples and historical circumstances. A person may be generally friendly to the free market but also be sympathetic to traditional ways of life and see these as potentially compatible with a market adapted to the needs of the particular people. The new Jacobin believes that democracy, with capitalism as an integral part, is not only the ultimate form of sociopolitical organization but that it should replace ancient institutions and habits. He uses the term "democracy" with great frequency and invokes democracy as the justification for virtually all action, international as well as domestic. This faith in democracy is closely tied to a desire for equality—the latter understood as the removal of old elites and old forms of social and cultural discrimination. These are seen as standing in the way of properly rewarding utilitarian and intellectual merit. The new Jacobin wants to replace traditional societies with "modern" societies modeled on what he takes to be universal principles. What many non-Western countries disdain and resist as "Western influence" is not so much traditional Western civilization as the kind of modern West that the new Jacobin favors and promotes. Interestingly, some of the political regimes that he especially opposes, in the Muslim world, for example, are not so much traditional as attempts at an indigenous political modernism of a non-Western type. The new Jacobin does not want competition in prescribing the right model. To contain or get rid of a particularly obstreperous and troublesome but quasi-modernistic regime he may be willing, in the Middle East, for example, to form an uneasy temporary alliance with a more traditional Islamic regime.

The new Jacobin is convinced that he knows what is best for all mankind, and if much of mankind shows reluctance to follow his lead, it is to him a sign that injustice, superstition, and general backwardness or a misconceived modernistic radicalism is standing in the way of progress. The new Jacobin is not content with voicing his own ideas and letting the peoples of the world make their own decisions. They must recognize the superiority of his principles. Governments that do not do so appear to him perverse. They are obviously based on oppression of the particular people. So strong is the zealotry of the new Jacobin that he wants the forces of democracy, and especially the United States, to use pressure tactics to make other countries conform. Even if various peoples of the world pose no threat to other states, they cannot be left to their own devices in deciding how to address their political needs. The world must be rid of unenlightened, undemocratic societies. If persuasion and diplomatic pressure fail, the forces of democracy should be willing to resort to military means, especially against powers that have the temerity of openly defying the United States. The new Jacobin desires strong, activist government that can enact what he considers virtuous purposes.

This general definition might seem generally to describe what is called "social democracy" or "social liberalism" in Europe and "liberalism" in the United States. This is a type of liberalism that has little in common with the kind of classical liberalism, today sometimes called libertarianism, that wants limited government of modest ambition, that finds equality incompatible with freedom and that is also not necessarily hostile to traditional societies. The typical modern American liberal, by contrast, stresses democracy and equality, desires big, activist government, and wants outdated regimes in the world to give way to progressive ones. Nevertheless, though many liberals are indeed prone to the kind of stance that is here called neo-Jacobinism, others are more pragmatic than ideological and do not entertain ambitious plans for reforming other societies. They are not trying to launch a worldwide crusade, buttressed by military power, in behalf of what they believe. In fact, many American liberals do not like the idea of the United States throwing its weight around. Like their European counterparts, they are more interested in preserving and improving what they think has been achieved in their own countries than in setting the rest of the world right. The presumption that Western liberal democracy with its elaborate welfare state is superior to all other societies is deep-seated in the liberal heart and mind, but often realism regarding the social circumstances of particular peoples together with a sense of history restrain the liberal inclination to prescribe for mankind as a whole. Sometimes liberals of much learning and general culture are qualified admirers of the old Western society and resist ideological nostrums. Liberals of this kind are not easily told apart from conservatives of similar sophistication. One may point, for example, to such major American figures in the mid-twentieth century as the theologian Reinhold Niebuhr, the theorist of international relations Hans Morgenthau, the columnist Walter Lippmann, the diplomat George Kennan and the Democratic presidential candidate Senator Eugene McCarthy.

In the last few decades those American liberals who are the most prone to a missionary, moralistic posture have come to form the core of what is today commonly called "neoconservatism." Many prominent intellectuals and political activists of that description worked for or were otherwise closely associated with liberal politicians in the Democratic party like the late Senators Henry Jackson, Hubert

Humphrey, and Daniel Patrick Moynihan, who were also strongly anti-communist. This long list includes William Bennett, Norman Podhoretz, Ben Wattenberg, Michael Novak, Elliot Abrams, and Richard Perle, persons who achieved prominence as public intellectuals and/or high public officials. They are today among the most ardent advocates of spreading democracy in the world through American assertiveness.

It is indicative of a lack of philosophical discipline and discrimination on the American right today that the neo-Jacobin impulse, which points away from old Western beliefs and points towards equality, destruction of traditional societies, and international crusading, should be so much in evidence among people called "conservatives." The impulse is especially strong among the neoconservatives. These intellectuals and political activists are in spite of their ideological label in many cases difficult to distinguish from modern liberals. What makes them distinctive is that they have come to question aspects of the earlier dominant American liberalism, not least the moral relativism with which it has commonly been associated, especially in American academia, and that they are strongly hawkish in foreign policy. The neoconservatives believe that the United States should revive the moral principles on which the country is based and be more affirmative internationally in promoting them. What especially connects many neoconservatives with neo-Jacobinism is the ideological intensity and political energy with which they advocate the spread of democracy and how they conceive of the universal principles that they promote. They advocate the latter on the basis of a general worldview. What makes many neoconservatives stand out in the context of this book is their crusading demeanor and that they, more than any other major intellectual and political group, are pursuing a long-term political strategy that includes a marked willingness to employ military means in advancing their cause. Because of the prominence of neoconservatives in the electronic and print media neoconservatism has become virtually synonymous in the public mind with conservatism, this in spite of sharp contrasts between aspects of neoconservatism and older American conservatism. The result is an abundance of paradoxes. For example, many who consider themselves conservative today believe that a conservative is always hawkish in foreign policy, whatever the circumstances.

Neoconservatives often speak of the need for reinvigorating "virtue" in America, a theme for which William Bennett, Ronald Reagan's secretary of education, has long been a leading and very visible spokesman. Their conception of virtue is not always unrelated to traditional Western notions of virtue, but one of its most prominent ingredients connects it with the Jacobin conception: Virtue is assumed to make Americans not so much willing to compromise with others as to make them politically insistent in spreading American principles; the effect of this virtue is to boost the moral earnestness and self-righteousness of those who would tell other countries how to conduct their affairs. When Bennett published *The Book of Virtues*, his best-selling anthology of edifying "moral stories" for children, one virtue, which has been central to the Western and American moral heritage, was conspicuously missing from those illustrated in his book, that of humility. [2]

Like liberals of the ordinary type, neoconservatives can be more or less prone to a neo-Jacobin outlook. A number of them will be quoted and discussed below who express neo-Jacobin sentiments in a particularly clear-cut and illustrative way. This is not to say that neconservatism equals neo-Jacobinism. Neoconservatism, as the term is ordinarily used, is too loose a constellation of individuals, is intellectually too diverse, and too much of a composite to make such a simple connection. In fact, the person who is often called the "godfather" of American neoconservatism, Irving Kristol, is not only not a very typical neoconservative but is not among those with the most pronounced neo-Jacobin leanings. But Kristol's son, William, clearly is (as will become evident below), though, like many other neoconservatives, he attempts to combine that strong ideological disposition with ideas less inimical to a traditional conservatism. Many columnists and other media commentators whose intellectual profile has clearly discernible neo-Jacobin features, consciously or unconsciously keep ultimately incompatible ideas together. One example among many is George F. Will, who has drifted further and further in the direction of democratism, especially in foreign affairs, but who is also trying to hold on to elements of a cultural and social conservatism. The same pattern is common among neoconservative writers of all kinds, from journalists to academics. Lack of philosophical sophistication sometimes facilitates rather odd combinations of ideas, as when fervent democratists attempt to make room also for fairly traditional Christian theological and social views.

A large number of newspapers, magazines, and journals promote or are highly receptive to a generally neo-Jacobin outlook without being wholly wedded to that point of view. The editorial and op-ed pages of the *Wall Street Journal*, the *Washington Post,* the *Washington Times* and, to a more limited extent, the *New York Times*, frequently give space to generally neo-Jacobin opinion, particularly on issues of foreign policy. Magazines that routinely publish articles in this same vein and that are increasingly difficult to tell apart with regard to their strong neo-Jacobin propensities are the *Weekly Standard*, *Commentary*, the *New Republic* and *National Review. U.S. News and World Report*, *Time*, and *Newsweek* are less intellectual but drawn to a similar outlook on America and the world. Though all of these publications also contain writing of different inspiration, they are markedly friendly to neo-Jacobin views. All of these newspapers and magazines exemplify the kind of intellectual confusion that was mentioned above, though, in the case of some, the presence of dissonant ideas within their pages may be due simply to a wish to publish different points of view. The financier of the *Weekly Standard*, the Australian Rupert Murdoch, is the owner of the Fox television network, which gives more prominence to neo-Jacobin opinion than any other network.

During the administration of President George W. Bush members of the so-called Christian right buttressed neo-Jacobin moralism with religious triumphalism. Departing emphatically from the traditional Christian view that no political cause can be identified with the will of God, they have assigned to America, led by a man of God, the task of doing God's will in the world, especially in matters related to God's chosen people, Israel. Having little or no influence on America's nationally dominant culture, this sectarian form of Christianity has, especially with regard to its foreign policy concerns, provided much grass roots political support for the neo-Jacobin cause, not least with regard to the question of war with Iraq.

A number of "leftist" or "progressive" publications, such as the *American Prospect*, the *Nation*, and the *Progressive* stand generally in the Jacobin tradition, but they are not attracted to what is perhaps the most distinctive feature of the new Jacobinism, which is to regard the United States as the embodiment of universal principles and to wish for the United States to spearhead the remaking of the world. Many American liberals are socialists in light disguise, and they are critical of "capitalist" America and the role of the United States in the world. They do not share the neo-Jacobin enthusiasm for free markets. The new Jacobins are also more obviously and systematically imperialistic and far more prone to favor military means to advance their goals.

Neo-Jacobinism cannot be said entirely to dominate any major think-tank or institute in the United States, but it has more than a foothold in a number of them. These include the Claremont Institute and the Hoover Institution on the West Coast and the American Enterprise Institute, the Institute on Religion and Public Life, the Ethics and Public Policy Center, and the Heritage Foundation on the East Coast. Each of these organizations has a wider intellectual scope and cannot easily be classified, but they have all been hospitable to the democratist persuasion. The American Enterprise Institute stands out as the most well-established and well-connected purveyor of such ideas. In the area of foreign policy, The Project for the New American Century, founded in 1997, has played a central role in spreading neo-Jacobin ideas outside and inside the U.S. government. The Project has gathered and coordinated the activities of a large number of mostly neoconservative intellectuals, political activists, and former or present public officials like Richard Cheney, Donald Rumsfeld, William Kristol, Richard Perle, and Paul Wolfowitz. The Project has helped propagate the ideology of American empire and translate it into a specific foreign policy strategy, including plans for war against Iraq. These efforts paid handsome dividends in the George W. Bush administration, which lifted many individuals from this circle into government and adopted most of its ideas.

One of several large charitable foundations that have looked with favor on individuals and projects of a neo-Jacobin type is the Bradley Foundation. A number of "leftist" think tanks and foundations are also favorable to Jacobin ideas, but, unlike the new Jacobins, they are not committed to virtue, capitalism and American international hegemony.

In the universities many of the professors who are drawn to a neo-Jacobin outlook were influenced by the political philosopher Leo

Strauss (1899-1973), long a professor at the University of Chicago, or by Strauss's immediate or second-generation disciples, including Allan Bloom, Walter Berns, Martin Diamond, Harry Jaffa, and Harvey Mansfield, Jr. Strauss's work is by no means unambiguous. It has elements that connect it with traditional Western moral and political beliefs. Strauss also cannot be held responsible for all of the uses to which his ideas have been put by many of his students and readers. Still, there is, as will be shown later, a clear connection between a Straussian anti-historical, abstract notion of natural right and the neo-Jacobin fondness for what it considers universal principles. Partly to establish this relationship, the ideas of Allan Bloom will be examined in some depth. His already mentioned book *The Closing of the American Mind* has a prominent neo-Jacobin component. Indeed, that book may come closer than any other work of political theory from recent decades to offering a quasi-systematic statement of the fundamental ideas of neo-Jacobinism, though that book, too, has ideas pointing in a different direction.

In the second half of the twentieth century, Leo Strauss and a steadily growing number of Straussian professors like Bloom created an intellectual movement of markedly sectarian and cliquish traits. They have by now transmitted their ideas to many thousands of students, many of whom think of themselves as belonging to a distinct intellectual elite. A high percentage of them have gravitated to college and university faculties, think tanks, journalism, and government, and many have reached very high positions.

Besides cultivating the belief that their insight makes them superior to any other intellectuals, to say nothing of the common people, Straussians have long fostered a both explicitly and implicitly conspiratorial mind-set. A part of the appeal of Strauss to members of this network of intellectuals has been his idea that only a few sophisticated minds can really understand and face the truth about politics. To protect themselves against the ignorant and to be able to influence the powers-that-be, the philosophers must, according to Strauss, hide their innermost beliefs and true motives, not least from rulers whom they want to advice. Following Plato's recommendation, the philosophers must tell "noble lies" that are more palatable to others than the truth. Strauss made a distinction between "esoteric" and "exoteric" writing in the history of political philosophy. What the philosophers profess publicly and on the surface forms their exoteric writings. Though the ideas formulated for general consumption may be partly or wholly disingenuous, they are designed to create the intellectual climate and other circumstances that will facilitate the philosophers' ascent to power. What they really think is revealed obliquely in esoteric writing accessible only to the sophisticated few. Pursuing their objectives, the insightful must surpass the deceit of their enemies. Having gained access to the ruler through dissimulation, sycophancy, and general craftiness, they are in a position to whisper in the ruler's ear, make him their instrument.

The mind-set just described is characteristic of a large number of intellectuals and political activists who are aware of each other as fellow Straussians. Members of this movement began to achieve important positions in government many years ago and were given an especially large role in the George W. Bush administration, which placed Straussians or their close allies in key positions as speechwriters, advisors, and major office holders, notably in the White House, the Pentagon, the State Department, and the staff of the vice president. The neoconservatives mentioned above either belong to or are closely aligned with this widening circle. Allan Bloom is just one Straussian professor to have encouraged his students to seek political influence and to have stayed in close touch with them as they followed this advice.[3]

Analysis of Straussian thinking is complicated by the fact that most Straussians do not quite know their own minds. Over time, their presumed intellectual deceptions and their innermost beliefs become closely intertwined and increasingly difficult to tell apart. Their deceptions become self-deceiving. Some Straussians think of themselves as moral nihilists deep down but are to some extent also persuaded by their own exoteric arguments in favor of natural right. Many others think of themselves as believers in moral universality but make some bows toward nihilism to seem subtle and shrewd in arguing the case for universalism. Having difficulty deciding what they really believe on the ultimate questions, many Straussians engage in elaborate intellectual contortions. What other philosophers may see as rather transparent confusion, they prefer to regard as well-nigh superhuman philosophical sophistication wholly beyond the grasp of the hoi polloi, the masses.

As will be shown, Straussianism has contributed much to the ideology of neo-Jacobinism as well as to its sectarian ways of thinking and operating. Yet even here it must be pointed out that no intellectual-political movement is univocal. Straussianism has its own intellectual divisions, and it contains divergent potentialities, some of them incongruent with neo-Jacobinism. In this book the emphasis will be on those elements of Straussianism, esoteric or exoteric, that did help shape neo-Jacobinism.

Needless to say, large numbers of intellectuals who do not have a reputation as conservatives or neoconservatives have generally Jacobin ideas for sweeping social, political, economic, and cultural change. They may be called "liberals," "leftists," "Marxists," "radicals," and so on. But these diverse individuals are usually different from the new Jacobins in that their rhetoric comes across as openly subversive of American society. The new Jacobins have managed to portray themselves as defenders of America, as believing in "moral values," and as having mainstream progressive views. This image of respectability has made it possible for the new Jacobins to play a significant role in the major political parties and the media and powerfully to affect America's domestic and international policies.

In sum, there is in America a large and very powerful intellectual-journalistic-political network within which neo-Jacobin thinking and activism is an often-decisive factor. Neo-Jacobin ideas help give the network its coherence and sense of common direction. It has access to enormous financial resources and has the power to shape public opinion and government policy.

It might be commented that, in comparison with communists and other radical leftists, the new Jacobins do not seem to be among the more extreme representatives of the Jacobin propensity. If one concentrates on the substance of declared policy and employs the conventional ideological spectrum, this point has merit, but it would be a mistake to assume that only self-proclaimed totalitarian socialists or fascists can be universalistic, imperialistic, and tyrannical, be driven by a desire to rule and conquer. In the West today and for the foreseeable future, especially in the United States, hard-line, orthodox socialism is highly unlikely to exercise much influence over domestic and foreign policy. The opposite is true of the new Jacobinism.

Among the original French Jacobins there were those, such as François-Noël Babeuf (1760-1797), known also by his pen name Gracchus Babeuf, who wanted to go as far in revolutionizing society as to abolish the institution of private property, but the Jacobins who controlled the French Revolution wanted to retain that institution, though in thoroughly modified form; they wanted property disentangled from traditional restraints and expectations and were hostile to the property arrangements of the hated old society. This difference of opinion among the Jacobins did not make the dominant Jacobins any less convinced of the absolute validity of their own beliefs or any less self-righteous in pursuing their cause. Like the old Jacobinism, the new Jacobinism is defined by its stated ideological preferences, but it is defined just as much by the belief that the world must be reshaped according to its ideas and by the intensity of its desire to have its own way. Its ideas can be understood in large part as a justification for a strong will to power. In keeping with this consideration, it is more important to know about a person whether he wants to impose his will on others than it is to know where exactly he fits on the simplistic and often misleading ideological spectrum of "left" to "right." In the end, perhaps the most distinguishing characteristic of Jacobinism is its lack of tolerance for other beliefs, especially ones rooted in long tradition. Exploring the ideas of the new Jacobinism is important partly for the light that it throws on the underlying wish to dominate.

Jacobins of all kinds are united in the desire to overturn the old world, but they favor different methods. Marxism was the radicalism of Jacobins who were excluded from the ruling circles of their societies. The new Jacobinism of contemporary America with its advocacy of capitalism and democracy is the Jacobinism of persons who feel their own power and think that they can dominate the society in which they live and use it for their own purposes. The new and the old Jacobinism share a desire for others to conform and a general anti-traditionalism. The latter element is masked somewhat in the case of the new Jacobins in that they are protective of the "tradition" of anti-traditionalism that originated in the Enlightenment and the French Revolution—one of the reasons that, superficially, they can seem conservative.

To be sure, there are in the United States plenty of leftists whose Jacobinism is in some respects more extreme than that of the new Jacobinism discussed in this book. The new Jacobins powerful today criticize these radicals for being enemies of America. Whereas the neo-Jacobins affirm America, *as they choose to interpret it*, these leftists heap abuse on the same country and call for its complete transformation, including the abolition of capitalism. These radicals are numerous and influential in the universities and the arts, and as the major trends in those fields are harbingers of things to come in the larger society, this form of Jacobinism is clearly a significant factor in the shaping of America's future. In Europe radical leftism is an even more potent force. Though the Jacobinism of these radicals is in some ways more virulent than that of the new Jacobins examined here, their obvious extremism and alienation from central political and economic institutions make it highly improbable that, in the first few decades of the twenty-first century at least, they will acquire an influence over American national politics and foreign policy that could match that of their more "moderate," if equally committed, counterparts. For all of their ideological and political militancy, they are very far from having the military might of the United States within their reach. Much more likely than that they will eventually acquire major political power is that most of them will be domesticated, co-opted, and integrated into an ideologically less obviously radical but equally purposeful and tenacious neo-Jacobin regime.

Whether new or old, Jacobinism wants a world of modern, progressive regimes. This does not mean that the new Jacobins reserve all of their hostility for the defenders of traditional societies. Like many radicals of the past, they direct some of their most intense hostility against those who claim to have a better formula for transforming the world than they do. The tensions between French Jacobins of different kinds was just mentioned. Another example of internecine feuds is the old conflict among communist factions, such as Trotskyists and Stalinists. More recently the neo-Jacobins clashed with communism, an ideology of a more obviously despotic and uncompromising cast but with which they nevertheless, as will be demonstrated later, have more in common than is obvious on the surface. Today, neo-Jacobins attack those on the left "who hate

America" while continuing to be hostile to defenders of traditional, pre-Enlightenment Western civilization.

The neo-Jacobins want the societies of the world to conform to what they consider the solely acceptable political and economic model. More specifically, they want to rid the globe of particular regimes that they call "rogue" or "evil," especially ones located in or having connections to the Middle East. One might comment, first of all, that no governments in the world are above criticism. Secondly, regimes disapproved by the neo-Jacobins can be positively noxious and brutal. In fact, some of them can be said to represent a form of Jacobinism of its own, for example, regimes in the Muslim world that are dominated much less by traditional Islam than by a modernistic secular socialism of the Baathist variety, or governments that are still communist in some sense. What will be said in criticism of neo-Jacobin international ambitions will contain no hidden implication that regimes challenged by the neo-Jacobins are unobjectionable. In the area of foreign affairs, what is at issue in this book is the danger of neo-Jacobin imperialism, which is all the more problematic in that it has access to the military, diplomatic and economic might of the only superpower in the world.

The states that neo-Jacobins want to attack or change typically pose little or no military threat to the United States or the rest of the Western world. As compared to the United States they have very modest military and economic resources. Neo-Jacobins warn repeatedly and excitedly about the danger of radical Islam, which they do without considering how the United States may have contributed to that danger. It is necessary to distinguish between defenders of the Western world who want carefully to monitor radical Islam and take precautions against its expanding and becoming more violent in its anti-Western attitudes and the new Jacobins, who treat these movements as if they posed a major and imminent military threat and as if terrorism had a military solution. The neo-Jacobins want the United States to take preemptive action to dislodge unfriendly regimes and sanitize entire regions of the world. It is indicative of the neo-Jacobin intolerance for opposition and deviance from their own preferences that, again, the United States usually has almost nothing to fear militarily from the regimes singled out for special criticism. It is appropriate to point out that America spends as much on its armed forces and related security needs as do all of the rest of the countries of the world put together. None of the "rogue" states or political leaders aspire to dominating the world or can do so rhetorically with any credibility. Of the many questionable governments and movements in the world today none has the kind of international reach and organization and the kind of resources that might make it a military threat to societies in other parts of the world. It is very different with the United States. Should it decide to throw its weight around, it has the capacity to threaten and make war on states far and wide. Under the leadership of the new Jacobins, it will have a strong inclination to do precisely that. As there will never be any shortage of less than acceptable regimes or of movements capable of terrorism, creating a better world is an endless task.

Thus, though the world would be better off without Jacobinism of all types, today the American variety has by far the greatest capacity for mischief. When it comes to being alert to troublesome trends in the world, it would seem that people in America and the rest of the Western world should be alert first of all to dangerous developments within their own societies and not divert attention from them by always complaining about unsatisfactory regimes elsewhere on the globe.

This book does not deny that America and the West are in some respects superior to other societies. Like other Western nations, the United States can contribute much to the wellbeing of other peoples, not merely by setting an example. Neither does this book assume that the United States has no responsibility for the rest of the world or that it must never intervene abroad unless directly and acutely threatened. A great power has great responsibilities and must protect farflung interests. Sometimes it may be compelled to act against egregious violations of accepted standards of international conduct, especially if those violations should bear directly on its own legitimate interests. The United States needs to have a prudent strategy for dealing with the many dangers and challenges of the contemporary world, including intensifying anti-American and anti-Western sentiments. Precisely because the United States cannot avoid playing a major international role, it needs to recognize that the first responsibility of any nation, as of any individual, is to examine self and to try alleviating the flaws of self. Though this thought is abhorrent to the new

Jacobins, Americans need to ask themselves whether any of the resentment toward the United States in the world may be due to short-sighted, unsophisticated, arrogant, or heavy-handed conduct in combination with American and Western moral and cultural decline. Hostility to the United States is often attributed to envy. Might this be yet another form of conceit? This is just the kind of self-scrutiny from which neo-Jacobin ideology excuses the United States. What is being analyzed in these pages as a highly ominous phenomenon is the widespread presumption that in all essential respects America is superior to all other countries and that it has a right and a mission to prescribe the destiny of all mankind, by military force if necessary. Neo-Jacobin doctrine goes far beyond advocating the kind of limited and discriminating attentiveness to the problems of the world that is proper for any great power. The doctrine assigns to the United States the goal of armed world empire and sanctions ambitious, proactive international crusading, and interventionism.

The above sketch of the new Jacobinism is broadly drawn and merely suggestive. A great deal more will have to be said to define it. The new Jacobinism badly needs to be distinguished from other strains of thought and sentiment that it may superficially resemble. It is often mixed in particular persons with less questionable, sometimes promising, ideas, which it prevents from coming into their own and from achieving greater clarity and depth. Many American neoconservatives, for example, have much to contribute toward a revitalization and development of traditional Western beliefs, but their being simultaneously drawn to neo-Jacobin thinking that ultimately militates against those same beliefs tends to vitiate or undermine their potential contributions.

This book will make no systematic effort to classify particular individuals as representatives of the new Jacobinism. Nor will it attempt any comprehensive analysis and assessment of particular writers. This study aims to identify, illustrate, and analyze a general ideological phenomenon, a powerful *tendency* of thought, imagination and action with its own distinctive logic and momentum. The new Jacobinism amounts to an entire worldview and a concomitant set of practical reflexes. The emphasis in this book will be on the "ideal type" of the new Jacobinism, as it were, recognizing that the ideological dynamic under examination need not be, indeed, rarely is, the whole truth about particular persons. In these pages the label "new Jacobins" is not meant to imply the existence of an ideologically uniform and tightly organized group of individuals, all of whom embody neo-Jacobinism and nothing else and all of whom agree on every important practical question. The old Jacobins' devotion to universal principles and passionate desire to remake society did not preclude intense disagreement on specific issues of policy. The new Jacobins are no different. The term will refer to a large and varied body of individuals whose basic outlook on central questions of life is shaped by strong neo-Jacobin leanings but who also may not place the same emphasis on each element of neo-Jacobin ideology. Particular individuals deserve the designation "neo-Jacobin" in proportion as they answer to the ideal type. The specific attributes of the ideal type will become clearer as the argument of this book unfolds.

Looking at the different components of the new Jacobinism, one might say, using a term from medicine, that they form a syndrome, that is to say, a pattern of symptoms that tend to go together.[4] These symptoms may be more or less pronounced in particular individuals, but in a full-blown case of the condition in question all of them are markedly present. It is understood that some intellectuals embrace the new Jacobinism in moderate or diluted form, while others give it purer expression. As already mentioned, the Jacobin ideological spirit also often coexists tenuously with beliefs that are ultimately hard to reconcile with it. Using another medical analogy, the new Jacobinism might be likened to a virus that strikes those hardest whose immune system is weak but has milder effects on those of healthier constitution.

The individuals who most clearly represent what is here called the new Jacobinism often have some more than marginal personal connection with extreme leftist political thought, for example, from having been Marxists. Now fashioning themselves champions of democracy and capitalism, they are still, like the Marxists, true believers, who make universalistic claims for their own beliefs and want to change the world accordingly.

The following chapters provide a number of distinctions and definitions. These are intended to clarify the condition of Western democracy and to explain the seriousness of the crisis in which it finds itself. The new Jacobinism can be seen as a structuring force, a common denominator, within a broader stream of ideas, sentiments, and practice that is today transforming Western society. This is not to deny that currents of different ideological origins play an important role in turning the West away from its older traditions, but the new Jacobinism is well financed, intellectually vigorous, journalistically and politically well connected and rather well organized around strategic objectives. Its ideological and political commitment is intense and persistent, and its influence in the media and in political-intellectual debate surpasses that of currents that may be more leftist in conventional ideological terms but that are also more unfocused and erratic as well as less "mainstream" in appearance.

The new Jacobinism has the wind at its back not because it has captured the most learned and mature minds of the Western world, but because its ideas are generally palatable to the zeitgeist and helpful to powerful financial and political interests. Philosophically it offers intellectuals of some education an alternative to moral nihilism and relativism. That some of the new Jacobins are themselves ultimately nihilists, and consider themselves such, is obscured by their nevertheless making a spirited defense of universal principles. The neo-Jacobin advocacy of an assertive foreign policy in behalf of democracy also appeals to people of more pragmatic but nationalistic outlook who like the idea of their own country being able to tell other countries how to behave. The democratist rhetoric of the new Jacobinism puts a nice gloss on the will to power.

Some of the individuals who will be quoted in this book as being in some ways representative of the neo-Jacobin mindset may have reputations as major thinkers among some academics and in various intellectual magazines, but they would not attract a great deal of interest among philosophers outside of the mentioned circles, were it not for their influence, name-recognition, and visibility. Their ideas will be examined here not because of their intrinsic philosophical importance—their primary appeal is not to the philosophical mind—but because explication and analysis of them will help demonstrate the meaning and practical import of the new Jacobinism. A number of persons who are not primarily scholars or thinkers but political journalists or activists of some prominence will be discussed or mentioned because they illustrate particularly well the ideological and political tenor of the new Jacobinism. To consider the views of such individuals is all the more appropriate as the objectives of the movement are decidedly and primarily political.

Notes

1.   William Kristol and David Brooks, *Wall Street Journal*, September 15, 1997.
2.   William Bennett, *The Book of Virtues* (New York: Simon and Schuster, 1993).
3.   In *Ravelstein,* the novel in in which Saul Bellow gives a lightly fictionalized biography of his old friend Allan Bloom, the narrator recalls Ravelstein receiving telephone calls from former students now in government. One such call was from a high official in the defense department during Desert Storm. According to Bellow, the former student conveyed highly sensitive information about the war, complaining that the president was not "completing the job" but leaving Saddam Hussein in power.
4.   The term "syndrome" is used similarly by James Burnham to classify ideas in his books *Suicide of the West* (New York: John Day Company, 1964) and *Congress and the American Tradition* (Chicago: Henry Regnery Company, 1965).

3

Creative Traditionalism or Radicalism?

"The true philosopher, . . . whose mind is on higher realities, has no time to look at the affairs of men, or to take part in their quarrels with all the jealousy and bitterness they involve. His eyes are turned to contemplate fixed and immutable realities, a realm where there is no injustice done or suffered, but all is reason and order, and which is the model which he imitates and to which he assimilates himself, as far as he can."—Plato[1]

This book will frequently compare Jacobinism, old or new, to that against which it rebels. Jacobinism will be contrasted with what can conveniently be summarized as "the Western heritage," "traditional society," "the old ethos," or the like. It should be made clear, and underlined, that this phraseology is not meant to imply that the older Western civilization against which the Enlightenment and the French Revolution reacted was all of a piece, uniform in regard to fundamental assumptions. For example, in classical Greek thought, Plato and Aristotle had very significant disagreements, and Christianity was always torn by doctrinal and other disputes. Neither is anything in this book intended to imply that the choice facing today's Westerners is between a Jacobin break with the ancient Western civilization inspired by Greece, Rome, and Christianity and a return to the ideas and practices of the past.

That it is not possible or desirable simply to revive the ways of an earlier era hardly needs proving. A revitalization or recovery of the older Western traditions would have to involve a rearticulation of old insights and values in new circumstances as well as a willingness to abandon some deep-seated beliefs. The task of rearticulation and adaptation would require a full and sensitive consideration of the best that has been wrought by Western modernity and the synthesizing of those elements with the ancient heritage. A continuation of the

43

Western traditions must of necessity be a reconstitution and development of earlier achievements. Even in historical periods of relative stability and continuity the words of Edmund Burke apply: "A state without the means of some change is without the means of its conservation." In a healthy civilization old and new must blend and shape each other: "The whole, at one time, is never old or middle-aged or young, but, in a condition of unchangeable constancy, moves on through the varied tenor of perpetual decay, fall, renovation, and progression."[2] If civilization is to maintain itself, it cannot be a mere imitation or repetition of old patterns. Tradition has to come alive in the here and now through the creativity of individuals who recognize both humanity's dependence on the best of the past and the needs and opportunities offered by changed circumstances. Without such individuals, tradition degenerates into deadening routine and antiquarian, merely formal traditionalism.

Many people who grieve the progressive destruction of Western civilization and are reluctant to adjust to what seems an ever more extreme and perverse "modernity" or "postmodernity" are tempted simply to escape from the realities of the present. They retreat into feelings of wounded piety, withdraw into the catacombs, as it were. The great "Tradition," often seen as originating in divine revelation, becomes a treasure of the past to be held in safekeeping for coming generations. Thus reified, the Tradition becomes a kind of fetish, which has little relevance to a world that will not conform and will not stand still. Considering the severity of the problems of the Western world, such attitudes of resignation should perhaps not be judged too harshly, but the many references in this book to the conflict between Jacobinism and Western civilization are not intended to suggest that the kind of society that would form the alternative to the Jacobin vision has its model or definition somewhere in the past. On the contrary, it is assumed here that, if traditional Western society is to be carried forward, it must be done through the kind of revitalization and reconstruction that has just been described. Indeed, some of the terms that express Jacobin ideology—"democracy," "equality," etc.—can have different meanings, some of which, although they emerge from considerations similar to those of the Jacobins, can be reconciled with the older Western view of man and society. Modernity, including the French Revolution itself, contains opposed potentialities, and some of these may be indispensable to the reinvigoration and healthy development of the Western world. Other potentialities of modernity, such as those appealing most to the Jacobin spirit, manifest a sharp, often hate-driven break with the ancient ways of the West. It should be kept in mind, thus, that the tension ultimately of concern in this book is not between old and new but between those ideas and practices of the modern world that are in actual or potential continuity with the ancient heritage of humane civilization and those that serve to destroy it.

One of the defining attributes of the old and the new Jacobinism is the belief that good social and political order has its source in ahistorical, abstract thinking. According to this view, mankind can, provided it makes full use of its rationality, generally speaking do without the historical heritage that Edmund Burke called "the general bank and capital of nations and of ages."[3] For Burke, a civilized society is the result of a slow, protracted, and often painful process of selection and accumulation. Much that builds order and well-being into life remains partly hidden from view. It is necessary, Burke argued, to approach historically evolved society with respect and humility as well as a critical eye and to be cautious in making changes. Innovation may do damage that the reformers in their preoccupation with their own favorite abstract ideas are not able to foresee. A belief that the reflection and experience of mankind carry no more weight in guiding society than the opinions in vogue in the present historical moment is, in Burke's view, superficial and dangerous. The old and new Jacobins disagree. They have a strong prejudice against tradition as being the depository of backward and irrational belief. Progress means to them rejecting "the bad old days" and relying on ahistorical, rational principles to set society's direction. To the extent that the new Jacobins respect "classical" thinkers, they interpret them as conforming in essential respects to their own intellectual leanings and as being Enlightenment figures before their time.

In the specifically American context, the new Jacobins do not identify with the political tradition that the Framers of the U.S. Constitution represented and that traces its origins far into an English and European past. They identify instead with certain principles that they deem universal and morally compelling, which they simply attribute to the Framers. As will be demonstrated later, the new Jacobins stress the more radical potentialities of America at the time of the War of Independence and the drafting of the Constitution. Their favorite "Founder" is Thomas Jefferson, whose picture of America was of a country ridding itself of an older political legacy. Though Jefferson was not wholly consistent in intellectual and practical orientation, he was quite untypical of the leading American political figures of his time in his dislike of the U.S. Constitution, his fondness for radical French ideas, his deep suspicion of elites, his populist majoritarianism and his ideological commitment to revolution as a way of ensuring good government. Even his defense of states' rights, which has endeared him to American conservatives, turns out to be due in large part to his championing the virtue of "the people." His thinking overlaps to a considerable extent with that of Rousseau. Jefferson appeals to the new Jacobins as one whose ultimate allegiance is to abstractly conceived rights or ideas rather than to concrete American traditions and ways of life.

There are good grounds for having reservations about the old Western traditions; even their strongest admirers recognize that they have significant flaws and see the need for revisions and supplements. At least some of the problems raised by the French Jacobins were real problems, only the Jacobins addressed them in a radical, uncompromising way, thinking that their own abstract ideas were the only proper model for society. The problems could have been understood and dealt with very differently. Individuals who think historically about civilization and who are friendly to, if not uncritical of, the old Western tradition see their role as strengthening rather than scuttling pre-Enlightenment civilization. As will be shown at considerable length, the new Jacobinism pursues a much different course.

The intellectual and moral confusion of the West today has obscured the broad range of possible motives for desiring change. One of the purposes of this book is to demonstrate that in this area appearances are often deceiving. It is essential to be able to distinguish between attempts to gut or obliterate old traditions and efforts to revise and develop them in new circumstances. Seemingly small and subtle differences in terminology can conceal large differences in meaning. Hence the emphasis in this book on distinctions, definitions, and contrasts.

Notes

1.   Plato, *Republic* (Harmondsworth: Penguin, 1987), bk. VI, 296-7 (501b-d).
2.   Edmund Burke, *Reflections on the Revolution in France* (Indianapolis, IN: Hackett Publishing Company, 1987), 19, 35.
3.   Ibid., 76.

4

Democracy: Plebiscitary or Constitutional?

" The great political leader is not content to whittle down his goals . . . He knows that archaic governmental routines cannot always be broken up by adjustment and adaptation . . . but by 'the application of overwhelming external force.'"
—*James MacGregor Burns[1]*

"Absolute acquiescence in the decisions of the majority [is] the vital principle of republics."—*Thomas Jefferson[2]*

A distinguishing characteristic of the new Jacobins is that they passionately advocate democracy and want to spread it to all parts of the world. They would like U.S. foreign policy to be committed to this objective. Still, these proponents of democracy do not pay much attention to the precise meaning of the term; they associate it vaguely with "equality," "human rights," and "majority rule." Their main purpose seems to be to gain forward momentum for their general cause by using a term that has favorable connotations, partly due to their own efforts. Democracy means in the end whatever they think is good for the world.

The neo-Jacobin promotion of democracy leaves all-important issues unaddressed. It neglects or conceals, specifically, that, as ordinarily defined by the new Jacobins, the mentioned principles are hard to reconcile with American constitutionalism. The latter has deep roots in Western Christian civilization in general and British culture in particular. A central objective of neo-Jacobin democratism is to sever the connection with old traditions and to put ideas of government on a new footing provided by ahistorical, enlightened rationality. Many of the new Jacobins intimate that certain classical thinkers provide support for their own ideology, which contributes to an appearance of conservatism, but they draw very selectively from those thinkers, take their ideas out of historical context and interpret them as forerunners of their own kind of thinking. When the new Jacobins advocate democracy, they think of it as a progressive force that clears away old religious, cultural, intellectual, and political beliefs and practices, much as the French Revolution and the Enlightenment sought to overturn the old European order.

To demonstrate the ideological and practical import of neo-Jacobin democratism it is necessary to make a distinction between two different forms of popular government. This distinction has been set forth at length elsewhere.[3] Here it will only be summarized. Although both notions of government are referred to as "democracy," they are not different versions of the same kind of government. They imply radically different understandings of human nature and society and have radically different institutional entailments. They are ultimately incompatible. The one may be called constitutional or representative democracy, the other plebiscitary or majoritarian democracy. The former is compatible with the old Western view of man's moral predicament. The latter flows from the kind of ideas that Rousseau and the Jacobins advocated. Constitutional democracy means popular rule under self-imposed restraints and representative, decentralized, institutions. Its aim is not to enact the popular wishes of the moment but to articulate what in American constitutional parlance is called the "deliberate sense" of the people. Plebiscitary democracy aspires to rule according to the popular majority of the moment. To ensure the speediest possible implementation of their wishes it seeks the removal of representative, decentralized and decentralizing practices and structures that limit the power of the numerical majority. Plebiscitary democrats recognize that, especially in large modern societies, the people need government officials, "representatives," to serve them, but the proper role of these officials is not to exercise independent judgment in determining the public interest. They should be agents of the people.

Constitutional democracy assumes a human nature divided between higher and lower potentialities and sees a need to guard against merely self-serving, imprudent, and even tyrannical impulses in the individual and the people as a whole. According to John Adams, who was a key figure in shaping early American political thinking, the people can be as tyrannical as any king. The Framers of the American Constitution gave no power to the people as a national entity and placed various restraints on the ability of majorities to get their way. So also did the Framers try to protect against the abuse of power by government officials by instituting checks and balances. In a constitutional democracy the people and their representatives adopt restraints on power to arm themselves in advance against their own moments of weakness and shortsightedness. In awareness of the flaws of human nature, they do not wish to be governed according to their own impulse of the moment. Sound government requires that the popular opinions of the moment be carefully scrutinized, sometimes that they be resisted by responsible leaders. The real, more considered, and enduring will of the people emerges over time through the interplay between popular opinion, as expressed in elections and public debate, and the informed, independent judgment of popular representatives.

The American Framers set up a government that, by the standards of their own time, had a strong bias in favor of popular consent. They can even be said to have created a special kind of democracy. To understand the Framers' conception of good government it is necessary, however, to remember that they had a very low opinion of what they called "democracy" or "pure democracy." They associated it with demagoguery, rabble-rousing, opportunism, ignorance, and general irresponsibility. One of their chief aims was to protect against such possible manifestations of popular government. While envisioning broad popular participation in politics, they sought to shield most of those charged with making decisions from the momentary popular will. Except in the case of the House of Representatives voters could affect the decisions of the national institutions of government only indirectly, and even the members of the House could, for the two years of their term of office act independently of their constituencies, should they see the need to do so. The Framers never contemplated universal suffrage in the modern democratic sense, expecting only male property-owners to participate in politics and voting. Fearful of the passions of popular majorities, they sought to create structures conducive to responsible articulation of the long-term interests of the people as a whole.

Plebiscitary democracy, by contrast, does not entertain any deep-seated suspicions regarding the popular desires of the moment. It regards the wishes of the majority at any particular time as the best expression of the people's will. That will should become public policy without delay. If the people need leadership, it is of a kind that tries to anticipate not yet fully formed popular wishes in order to speed their enactment.

The two conceptions of democracy entail sharply different understandings of what constitutes a society and a people. Constitutional democracy assumes a decentralized society in which the lives of most citizens are centered in small, chiefly private, and local associations, what the late Robert Nisbet called "autonomous groups."[4] These can exercise independent authority. In the decentralized society there are many centers and levels of power. Political authority is widely dispersed, enabling regional and local entities to decide for themselves. American federalism and American tradition in general exemplify the decentralized sociopolitical structures of constitutional democracy. In such a society the citizens participate in and are shaped by communal relations that are concrete, specific, and local. People tend to define their own interests not as discrete individuals but as members of the groups that they most treasure, starting with the family and other associations at close range. By the "people," then, constitutional democracy does not mean an undifferentiated mass of individuals, whose will could be obtained by simply counting up votes according to the formula "one-man-one-vote." This numerical method disregards the social and qualitative ties between individuals. It ignores the fact that most people express their humanity and find their deepest satisfaction in associations of various kinds and that their interests as members of social subdivisions deserve consideration. Constitutional popular rule recognizes the need for adjusting government structures and elections to an expected diversity and proliferation of interests and to particular local circumstances.

Plebiscitary, majoritarian democracy takes the politically most significant meaning of "the people" to be the undifferentiated mass of individuals. Government should serve the national majority, whose will is ascertained by numerical, merely quantitative methods. Fifty percent plus one should rule. The measure of good democracy is that the popular majority has effective control over public policy.

Regional and local interests should be wholly subordinated to the majority of the most comprehensive political entity. The political dynamic of plebiscitary democracy is to mobilize, expand, and centralize government. The effect is to erode local and private autonomy and initiative and to efface what is locally and regionally distinctive.

It needs to be added that the dichotomy between two ultimately incompatible forms of democracy is but a part of a more comprehensive dichotomy that takes account of incompatible views of human life. The significance of the contrast between constitutional and plebiscitary popular rule becomes clearer when that distinction is related to a number of analogous and closely related distinctions. These distinctions elaborate different aspects of larger contending notions of man and society. Among the many terms that can be dichotomized in ways analogous to the dichotomy of the word "democracy" are "liberty," "capitalism," and "free market." Dichotomies of these terms make explicit meanings that lie implicit in the distinction between constitutional and plebiscitary democracy as well as in each of the other distinctions. As in the case of "democracy," great theoretical and practical confusion often hides behind the words "liberty," "capitalism," and "free market," each of which contains opposed potentialities. Like "democracy," these words have possible meanings that connect them with the Jacobin desire to overturn traditional societies. One of the reasons why the new Jacobinism is often able to find support in what would appear to be unexpected places is the failure of those who like the sound of these general terms to ascertain what they mean in the particular case. The terms sorely need to be dichotomized.

Notes

1.   James MacGregor Burns, *Uncommon Sense* (New York: Harper and Row, 1972), 175.
2.   Thomas Jefferson, *The Life and Selected Writings of Thomas Jefferson*, ed. Adrienne Koch and William Peden (New York: Modern Library, 1944), 324.
3.   See Claes G. Ryn, *Democracy and the Ethical Life*, second expanded edition (Washington, DC: The Catholic University of America Press, 1990).
4.   Robert Nisbet, *The Quest for Community* (San Francisco, CA: Institute for Contemporary Studies, 1990; first published in 1953).

5

Contrasting Forms of Morality and Society

"He who dares to undertake the establishment of a people should feel that he is, so to speak, in a position to change human nature, to transform each individual . . . into a part of a larger whole from which this individual receives, in a sense, his life and his being; to alter man's constitution in order to strengthen it."
—*Jean-Jacques Rousseau[1]*

Political institutions and practices are always a manifestation of a view of human nature and society. To understand particular conceptions of government is therefore always a matter of exploring their moral and other presuppositions. To do so is to discover that some seemingly dissimilar beliefs and arrangements are actually closely related, different dimensions of one and the same attempt to realize a certain notion of what life ought to be. One such connection is that between constitutional democracy and social and political decentralization. They are integrally related. Both of them reflect and express in concrete particulars a certain view of the fundamental needs of human nature. Life in a decentralized society with a proliferation of small and vigorous groups tends to foster habits of self-restraint and concern for others. It thereby helps create and maintain a moral disposition on which constitutional democracy depends in the long run. Most generally, a decentralized society shapes an entire attitude towards life, a way of thinking about how to deal with human beings at home, in the local community, in the nation, and abroad.

In the West, the decentralized society is deeply rooted in Christian ideas of community and virtue, which are akin to earlier Greek ideas, especially those of Aristotle. The individual's primary moral responsibility is to make the best of self and to love neighbor. This is a demanding notion of virtue, for nothing is more difficult than overcoming one's own selfishness and behaving charitably toward people of flesh and blood at close range. People with names and faces have a way of presenting us with concrete and immediate obligations. Sometimes they make highly uncomfortable demands on our time and energy. To make charitable behavior even more difficult, they may be our competitors, perhaps also difficult and unlikable. Moral responsibility is achieved only slowly and with effort. It is in daily life, primarily in one's own intimate associations, that opportunities for love of neighbor are actually present. Man's moral character is shaped and tested first and foremost in relationships that are up close and personal.

Virtue manifested as love of neighbor may be contrasted with what is perhaps the most common modern idea of virtue. The latter lets individuals claim moral worth who show no particular signs of moral character in their actual personal conduct and who may, by traditional moral standards, actually be odious and hard for people to live or work with. Their putative virtue is that they entertain benevolent sentiments towards various abstract entities, such as "the people," "mankind," "the proletariat," "the poor," "the downtrodden," "the starving third world," or the like—entities that are all diffuse and distant from the emoting person and which therefore impose on the individual no concrete and personally demanding obligations. Unlike the older notion of charity, the new virtue does not place any uncomfortable duties directly in front of the person. Those large collectives could not possibly be cared for by the individual; the task must be entrusted to government or some other large, well-funded, and well-equipped agency. Still, this sentimental posture of caring contains a pleasant ingredient of self-applause. It is, as it were, morality made easy. It presupposes no difficult improvement of self, no ability to behave well in actual human relationships.

Traditional Western morality creates a strong presumption that man's primary moral obligation is to deal with problems at close range, starting with self. The individual is acutely aware of his own weaknesses, aware that much needs to be done to remedy them. Doing well by family, kindred, friends, and colleagues is in itself a demanding task. If this task does not consume the moral energy of the individual, other heavy and pressing responsibilities await most human beings rather close to home and workplace. These should be attended to before presuming to tell people at a great distance how to live. We demonstrate our capacity for humanity in acts of character that take place chiefly within the concrete relationships of daily life. This attitude has been a central feature of the ethos of the decentralized society. The people most immediately touched by problems or opportunities are thought to have the main responsibility for acting on them.

The assumption that much needs improving *here* before turning attention elsewhere has shaped a corresponding attitude toward international relations: a country's primary duty is to conduct its own affairs and repair its own flaws. An interest in neighboring countries and the rest of the world comes naturally to any civilized society; the benefits of contacts across borders are numerous and varied: commercial, cultural, political, and military. But the effect of the old morality of character is to build self-restraint and respect for others into these relationships and to reduce the danger of conflict. The emphasis on curbing arrogance, greed, and other types of self-indulgence increases the chances for harmonious relations. A country has no reason to interfere militarily or otherwise with other countries except to protect its own vital interests and defend itself against threats.

The consequences of the fading of the old moral ethos are profound and far-reaching. The modern substitution of a sentimental, abstract love of mankind for personal character has shifted the burden of moral responsibility away from individuals, groups, and local communities. No longer is it assumed that most people's primary obligation is to individuals within the person's daily life. Morality should be focused on the wider world. This is how a person is thought really to show what he is morally worth. To the extent that people in the West have come to associate virtuous striving with great causes beyond local and daily life, they have begun devoting less energy to making the best of the here and now. Personal behavior towards "neighbor" seems to matter so much less than what must be done for those large needy collectives. Because of a changed notion of virtue, obligations have shifted from individuals in their families and communities to government, which has expanded greatly and become highly centralized. It is now widely believed that a person demonstrates morality by wishing to order other people's lives according to allegedly benevolent political schemes. The stronger and more ambitious that wish, the greater the evidence of virtue. Domestically, this morality places people under the administrative supervision of government. Internationally, it provides a mandate for telling other countries what is good for them.

It is important to understand that the older ethos now being pushed back is no mere abstract idea or ethereal sentiment. On the contrary, whether it influences private, local, national, or international conduct, it is a disposition of character that shapes individual conduct and manifests itself in sociopolitical structures in a wide range of concrete ways. Similarly, the weakening of that ethos has large and tangible consequences that are not confined to certain parts of social life. Not only government but also every other social institution and structure is transformed by the change. Democracy becomes very different depending on the presence or absence of the old Western moral ethos. But the same is true for freedom, capitalism, and other social phenomena. Just as the form and substance of government will vary with the personalities of those who make decisions, so in the marketplace, for instance, the content of supply and demand, the manner of competition, and the organization of business will be different depending on the outlook and character of those who produce and consume.

Note

1.   Rousseau, *Social Contract*, bk. II, ch. VII, 163.

6

Aristocratic and Anti-Aristocratic Democracy

"The American Constitutions—state and federal—that resulted from the . . . revolution had no *monarchial or aristocratic elements."—Harry Jaffa[1]*

Whether old or new, Jacobinism regards equality as the only legitimate basis for a just society. It has a deep prejudice against historically evolved social and political structures that place particular social groups or families in a position to act as arbiters of what is high and low and to decide what other individuals are worthy of advancement. The word "aristocratic" carries for the Jacobins unpleasant connotations, conjuring up images of arrogance, stupidity, narrow-mindedness, ignorance, and intolerance. Although Jacobin intellectuals consider themselves much superior to the common run of humanity and are anxious to lead "the people," their official doctrine is that no preconceived ideas should stand in the way of individuals moving up and achieving greater influence. What the new Jacobins find particularly objectionable are the kind of elites that were found in the old Western society, elites consisting in part of persons who had not achieved positions of influence through struggle and merit but had been more or less born to them—the kind of elites who also did not regard utilitarian effort and skill, intellectual smarts, or money-making ability as sufficient for entering the higher strata of society and politics. The Jacobins' ardent advocacy of equality seems to be to a considerable extent related to a wish to clear away obstacles to their own ascent to power.

In America, the neo-Jacobin preoccupation with equality produces a strong bias in the interpretation of the U.S. Constitution and the so-called "Founding." Hoping to take advantage of the old American reverence for the Constitution, the new Jacobins try to portray it as being in tune with their own notions of equality and democracy. Before this subject is discussed at length it is desirable to indicate in general terms how the neo-Jacobin mind-set clashes with the older conception of leadership and with the leadership envisioned by the Framers of the U.S. Constitution.

The view of human nature and morality that helps generate the decentralized, group-oriented society from which constitutional democracy is indistinguishable also fosters the kind of citizenship and leadership on which this same government depends. Only people who are used to self-discipline and respect for others can sustain a form of government in which the citizens must accept the restraint of law and accommodate different interests. In a democracy, the largest possible number of people are supposed to participate in governing. A person of bad character and other flaws is poorly equipped to rule self, to say nothing of exercising influence over others by voting or holding office. High morality cannot be expected to set the tone in any society, but more than any other form of government a democracy depends for its success on a citizenry with standards of conduct above the ordinary. A democracy also stands in special need of leadership by people of proven character and ability.

According to the old Western view, responsible behavior gets its start at home and in nearby associations. A capacity for leadership may eventually be demonstrated in the wider local community. There the individual remains under rather close scrutiny. Potential leaders stand out partly as moral examples. In traditional Western society it was assumed that people worthy of special political influence would have proven themselves in concrete action within their own sphere of life and work. They would have a good reputation built on long observation by peers. They would be admired and pushed forward by others not solely because of skill in their professional roles but because they had moral rectitude, civilized manners, prudence, honesty, moderation, modesty, strength of will, leadership ability, and so on. A good, responsible leader would be known not by professions of high virtue, but by human qualities actually demonstrated. Indeed, suspicions attached to individuals facile with noble-sounding phrases. A genuinely good person would not talk about his moral merit—humility would incline him against it—and there would, in any case, be no need for him to do so. People assumed that, preferably, power should be given to persons of moral substance and the right insight and experience. The implication of these observations for democracy, where most people are to have a share in government, is that the obligation to act responsibly must be widely accepted and encouraged.

Plato was one of democracy's sharpest critics, but he never recognized the possibility of what has here been called constitutional democracy. In the terms here employed he only acknowledged the possibility of plebiscitary, majoritarian democracy. Rule by the common people under leaders who cater to their desires is, Plato averred, inherently destructive of high moral and intellectual standards and inherently subversive of social order. Plato associated democracy with undisciplined, irresponsible freedom. It follows the desire currently strongest in the people, just as the soul of the democrat follows the whim of the moment. Democracy establishes equality of pleasures and of individuals. Those gain political power who most successfully pander to popular impulse. According to Plato, democracy destroys the last vestiges of aristocratic moral and intellectual order and ushers in the brutal lawlessness of tyranny. That in a civilized society the people might become more capable of self-rule through self-discipline and that a democracy might put limits on the majority and mitigate the drawbacks of popular government by incorporating aristocratic features would have been for Plato a very far-fetched, wholly implausible notion. Because it lets the common people have a say in government, democracy is for him by definition the lowest form of rule, except for the tyranny for which it prepares the way. Democracy is incompatible with the higher aspirations of human society. But the possibility of a special form of popular rule that Plato never considered was taken very seriously by the American Framers.

Aristotle was more receptive than Plato to broader participation in governing, but he took a similarly dim view of what he called "democracy." It was for him one of the bad regimes that should be strenuously resisted. Yet a regime that gives some power to the common people can be made tolerable by balancing their interest against the interest of other groups, notably that of the wealthy. All good regimes, Aristotle contended, manage to accommodate different groups while serving the common good. One such regime is "aristocracy," which means not rule by noblemen but rule by "the best," by individuals of high moral integrity and wisdom, who may also be members of long established leading families. The strengths of aristocrats are due in significant part to protracted shaping of the will, the mind, and the imagination, not least through formal education up to a high level. According to the ancient Greek definition, the aristocrat is a person who embodies the life of the good, the true, and the beautiful and who is therefore capable of true "friendship" with others. For Aristotle, the best ruler is not, as for Plato, a philosopher and a contemplative, but a philosophically and otherwise educated man of practical sense and experience. He is a natural leader and model for others. For any regime to be acceptable, it must make room somehow for the aristocratic spirit, which is needed to protect the common good against the blatant self-seeking and other destructive behavior of various groups.

Ancient Athens is said to be the "cradle of democracy." It should be mentioned in passing that this way of speaking is highly misleading in as much as people today make assumptions about democracy that are very different from those of the ancient Athenians. Modern democracies cover a far greater territory than Athens and have far greater populations, which requires rule by popular representatives in distant places. The relative intimacy of Athenian national politics is hard for a person from a modern Western society to imagine. Also, as understood by the Athenians, a democracy did not come even close to observing universal suffrage. Only a rather small minority of the population were considered candidates for political participation in a democratic period: the males who had been born in Athens and were of recognized Athenian ancestry. Women did not participate in politics. Neither did the very large part of the population that was made up of resident aliens. They were probably more numerous than the Athenians themselves but did not have naturalization available to them. The slaves, who ranged in employment from public servants to manual laborers, may have been about fifteen percent of the population. Thus, even in the most democratic of times, those who were considered eligible for political participation, that is, voting in the all-powerful popular assembly and holding office, may have been no more than about ten percent of the population. Though Athenian democracy was in important ways egalitarian and direct, the exclusive character of the participation in politics establishes a major contrast with modern Western democracies.[2]

Constitutional democracy as defined in this book can be seen as an attempt to realize freedom under law by building aristocratic traits into popular government. It does so by encouraging and drawing upon self-control, wisdom, and high experience among the citizens and upon the social structures that devotion to the higher life engenders. Political institutions and processes are deliberately shaped in ways that are expected to increase the likelihood that persons of character and insight will be influential. The original American Constitution provides many examples of an effort to counteract the dangers of plebiscitarianism, what the Framers scorn as "democracy." The Constitution give no power whatever to a numerical national majority; the American people have political standing *only* as members of political subdivisions, such as states and state electoral districts. The Constitution also places various checks on the authority it does grant to the people. Popular opinion is sifted through representative institutions. In the words of Federalist No. 10, it is desirable "to refine and enlarge the public views, by passing them through the medium of a chosen body of citizens, whose wisdom may best discern the true interest of their country."[3] The Framers also assumed that voting would be restricted to individuals who, as property owners, were expected to act more responsibly than others. To increase the odds of well-informed, responsible decisions the Framers deliberately shielded many officeholders from the pressures of popular opinion. Senators and presidents would be elected only indirectly by the people. According to the original Constitution, U.S. senators would be chosen by the state legislatures. The task of selecting a president was not entrusted to the American people in general, but was placed in the hands of the Electoral College. This body was intended to be composed of individuals of high standing in their states who would understand the requirements of the office of president and also be able to distinguish between presidential contenders of integrity and ability and ones of questionable character and ambition. Senators and presidents were given fairly substantial terms of office, making it easier for them to follow their own best judgment. Members of the Supreme Court would be even further removed from popular pressures. Appointed by the president with the consent of the Senate, they could serve for life and decide cases without fear of popular or other retribution. A similar prejudice against rash, partisan, or uninformed opinion was expected to be manifested in state and local checks on political power and in social structures generally. For a long time the American people were comfortable with the thinking of the Framers and sanctioned aristocratic or quasi-aristocratic institutions and attitudes as appropriate to articulating and promoting their own enduring will.

Contrary to the neo-Jacobin view of the American Constitution, it could even be plausibly argued that, in all but name, the Framers set up an elective constitutional monarchy with a quasi-aristocratic Senate and Supreme Court. According to the original Constitution, a president could have stayed in office for life, with the approval of the presidential electors at four-year intervals. Anger with the British king had produced much anti-royalistic rhetoric, but for all of the use of the term "republic," the Framers admired and hoped to replicate George Washington, whose demeanor and sense of decorum as president were more royal than republican. Though unintended, the power of the American president would in time far exceed that of most kings. Titles of nobility were prohibited by the Constitution, but the Framers hoped all the same that a special class of leaders would be nurtured and empowered who would be equipped to discern the best interest of the American people.

It is appropriate to consider here that the so-called "American Revolution" was not a revolution in the ordinary modern sense of that term. Though the Americans severed the political ties with England and though Tories and other British loyalists were purged or driven away, no radical social or political upheaval took place. America was not turned upside down. It continued largely as before, under partly different political management. Religious, educational, economic, and other habits and structures remained largely intact. For example, a large majority of those who signed the U.S. Constitution in 1787 were Episcopalians, that is to say, members of the church that in America carried forward the theology, liturgy, and other traditions of the Church of England. Far from indicating a desire for a break with the ways of England and Europe, the cultural habits of Americans after 1776 continued to show a pronounced Anglophile bias and an admiration for European traditions. One need only look to the architectural tastes of Americans embodied in homes, places of business, and public buildings that were built in the decades after 1776, to say nothing of the fondness for classical Greek and Roman styles. Even politically, there was a great deal of continuity between America before and after "the Revolution." In the states, already well-established institutions of self-government were retained or developed in newly written constitutions.

Given modern terminology, "the American Revolution" is a misnomer. The events in question are more accurately named "the War of Independence." The rebellion was undertaken not in the name of radical, abstract, universal principles, though a few Americans sometimes used this kind of rhetoric, but in protest against concrete and specific maltreatment of the colonies, notably, that of denying their residents their inherited "rights of Englishmen." These rights were now reclaimed, and the former colonies continued to exhibit not only the homegrown social and political patterns characteristic of the colonies but much of English tradition, including the Common Law. The Constitution adopted in 1789 bears the distinctive imprint of the American Framers, to be sure, but it also shows the continuing influence of the English and Western past. The Bill of Rights added to the Constitution was in large measure a codification of key elements of the Common Law.

Those today who like to stress the revolutionary nature of America's beginnings simply ignore an abundance of historical evidence. They are clearly pressing an ideological cause. There will be reason below to examine arguments of that kind at some length. It will be demonstrated further that early American constitutional republicanism had little in common with the ideology of democratism. The Framers were uninterested in plebiscitary rule. To the extent that they considered it at all, it was to point out and warn against its dangers. The proximity in time between the adoption of the U.S. Constitution and the start of the French Revolution might suggest that these were ideologically kindred events, but the American political mind that conceived the Constitution had formed long before the French Revolution and along lines very different from those of the French Jacobins. This American mind was steeped in old English and European civilization, specifically Christianity, though, it goes without saying, it had new, specifically American ingredients. Jacobin ideas played little role in America at the time, and the French Enlightenment was slow to impact America. A rather different kind of Enlightenment, the Scottish, was more influential. It did not have the French Enlightenment's pronounced animus against traditional society and was more easily reconciled with older types of thought.

Among the many factors that shaped the political views of the Framers were, to summarize, British constitutionalism and the Common Law with its procedural rights, a distinctive and concrete colonial experience permeated by religious faith, a tradition of localism and dispersed and decentralized power, belief in the importance of popular consent, a strong preference for deliberation, a belief in representative institutions, and, perhaps as important as anything else, modest expectations of government and politics due to the belief in original sin.

Though plebiscitarianism did not appreciably affect the Framing, it did have some defenders from the beginning, though not of the most radical Rousseauistic type. The most prominent and influential was Jefferson. He was and remained dissatisfied with the Constitution, which had been written in his absence, during his tenure as American minister to France. Like the French ideologues for whom he had an affinity, Jefferson was a committed believer in "the people" and in the need for cleansing government periodically of their enemies. He passionately defended majoritarianism. Sounding much like Rousseau, he advocated the "absolute acquiescence in the decisions of the majority—the vital principle of republics."[4] But even Jefferson had his constitutionalist side, and he, too, was in favor of a property requirement, though small, for voting. Moreover, his populist and other theorizing were often contradicted by his practice.

Plebiscitarian ways of thinking and acting have gained much ground in America since the time of the writing of the Constitution. Traditional political institutions have been gradually transformed by changing practice and by constitutional amendment and interpretation. They have also come under mounting intellectual assault. Some neo-Jacobin critics who do not wish to appear hostile to the Framers reinterpret the Founding as being far more majoritarian and egalitarian and far less shaped by old European, English, and American traditions than might appear. The Founders of America, they assert, started afresh on the basis of ahistorical rationality and universal principles. America was born out of revolution, much as the French Revolution overturned the old European order and set a brand new course. Many intellectuals in the United States who are hostile to the old Western and American society are more straightforward. They reject the Constitution and other American traditional institutions outright as being "elitist" and inimical to real democracy.[5]

The change in America's national political institutions since the adoption of the Constitution amounts to a far-reaching erosion of state and local autonomy and a huge expansion and centralization of power. After the Constitutional Convention of 1787 the defenders of the proposed constitution dismissed fears that the new central government might expand beyond the powers delegated to it and begin to undermine the sovereignty of the states. To reassure critics and to make it even more certain that the federal government would be restricted to the very limited functions enumerated in the original Constitution, the 10th Amendment was added: "The powers not delegated to the United States by the Constitution, nor prohibited by it to the states, are reserved to the states respectively, or to the people." Yet the federal government has expanded far beyond the worst fears of the early critics of the Constitution. Today scarcely any sphere of American life is exempt from federal power. The 10th Amendment is a dead letter.

It is only superficially a paradox that this enormous expansion and centralization of federal power should have been accompanied and in large part driven by ever-growing demands that more power be given to "the people." Whatever the theory of plebiscitary, majoritarian democracy, in practice it centralizes government and places more power in the hands of elites, those, specifically, who claim to act for the people. These elites are increasingly able to condition the desires of the masses and to persuade them of the need for yet more assistance from the central government, a process that is at the expense of private, local, and state autonomy.

The extent of the transformation of America's political and social institutions is obscured by philosophical confusion and lack of historical knowledge. In particular, the failure to make the all-important distinction between constitutional and plebiscitary popular rule has resulted in an inability to see what has really happened and how much is at stake.

It needs to become much better understood that government is indistinguishable from the moral, intellectual, and cultural conditions that give it shape and direction. Government manifests the preferences of an entire civilization. The transformation of American political thought and practice forms part of developments that encompass social life as a whole. If a reordering of moral priorities and a corresponding new self-understanding of Americans are changing American government, so are they changing intellectual, cultural, and economic life.

It should be reiterated that the distinction between two forms of popular government, one compatible and one incompatible with aristocratic self-control and responsibility, implies other distinctions between opposed potentialities of human life. Again, terms like "liberty," "private property," or "free market," have to be dichotomized no less than "democracy." Central to the needed dichotomies is the extent to which particular understandings of the mentioned terms emphasize or de-emphasize the importance of moral and other discipline and the kind of social and political structures from which they are indistinguishable. To what extent is an aristocratic element included? Without the proper distinctions, it is not possible meaningfully to classify advocates of "liberty," "private property," or "the free market." Like "democracy," these terms may hide meanings that are sharply at odds with the old Western ethical and cultural ethos and may actually stand for a burning wish to overturn traditional society. The extent of the transformation of America and of the larger civilization to which it belongs is partly hidden by the vague and uncritical use of general terms. The same confusion makes it possible for the new Jacobins to conceal objectives that, if they were wholly transparent, would generate greater opposition.

The next chapter will explore in greater depth the meaning of plebiscitary democracy, so that democratism with its glorification of "the people" can be more fully differentiated from constitutional popular government with its attempted incorporation of aristocratic features.

Notes

1.   Harry Jaffa, "Equality as a Conservative Principle," in William F. Buckley, Jr. and Charles R. Kessler, eds., *Keeping the Tablets* (New York: Harper & Row, 1988),

2.   For a treatment of the forms and circumstances of Greek democracy, see Sir Ernest Barker, *The Political Thought of Plato and Aristotle* (New York: Dover Publications, 1959), esp. 446-65.

3.   Alexander Hmilton, John Jay and James Madison, *The Federalist*, George W. Carey and James McClellan eds., (Dubuque: Kendall/Hunt Publishing Co., 1990), 47. 86.

4.   Jefferson, *Life and Selected Writings*, 324. For more on Jefferson as a majoritarian democrat, see Ryn, *Democracy*, esp. ch. XI.

5.   For a discussion of the moral, intellectual, and cultural roots of the American Framers, see Forrest McDonald, *Novus Ordo Seclorum: The Intellectual Origins of the Constitution* (Lawrence: University Press of Kansas, 1985) and Russell Kirk, *The Conservative Constitution* (Washington, D.C.: Regnery Gateway, 1990).

7

The Father of Democratism

"Man was born free, and everywhere he is in chains."—Jean-Jacques Rousseau[1]

"So long as several men together consider themselves to be a single body, they have but a single will."—Jean-Jacques Rousseau[2]

The ideas of Jean-Jacques Rousseau have been seminal for Western political and cultural radicalism. They were a decisive influence behind the most uncompromising attack on Western civilization in the eighteenth century. Since then Rousseau has contributed mightily to a transformation of the Western mind, imagination, and moral sensibility.[3] Directly or indirectly, he has inspired a large number of radical or revolutionary thinkers and actors.

To consider the moral and political ideas of Rousseau is appropriate here for several reasons. Most generally it will throw light on major trends in the Western world since his time. Understanding Rousseau is also essential to grasping the full import of the distinction between constitutional and majoritarian popular rule. It helps bring into relief the incompatibility between constitutionalism of the American type and a Jacobin-style faith in "the people." Further, examining Rousseau's ideas in some depth discloses the origins of the moralistic righteousness of the French Jacobins. The fact that most of the intellectual leaders of the new Jacobinism look with favor on Rousseau makes it all the more important to grasp the thrust of his thinking. These new Jacobins may not agree in all particulars with the interpretation of Rousseau here offered, but their fondness for him, however qualified, is a highly significant indication of what animates their ideology of democratism.

If traditional American constitutional government answers to the idea of constitutional popular rule, the idea of plebiscitary democracy is advocated in its purest form by Jean-Jacques Rousseau.[4] Starting from a belief in the natural goodness of man, Rousseau rejected the old belief that human nature needs moral and other restraints. Traditional civilization enslaves man to structures of inequality and artificiality. By completely destroying the old society, the people can form a new community of equality and brotherhood. As natural inclinations are liberated in the people they develop a common will. What Rousseau called the general will is to be expressed by the majority. Since this will is inherently good, it should be subject to no legal or other checks. Popular sovereignty must be unrestricted. The popular will of the moment must be a law unto itself. "Yesterday's law does not obligate today," Rousseau wrote. He dismissed constitutional and legal limits on the majority. It would be "absurd," he asserted, for the people to put over itself a law it could not break. "There neither is nor can be any type of fundamental law that is obligatory for the people as a body."[5] Rousseau thus collides head on with advocates of constitutionalism, such as the Framers of the U.S. Constitution, who subject not only the leaders of the people but the people themselves to substantial checks that are not easily changed or repealed.

In the *Social Contract*, Rousseau utterly rejected the idea that representatives should help articulate the popular will. The sovereign people "cannot be represented by anything but itself."[6] While the people may wish to entrust the *implementation* of their wishes to faithful government officials, representation in the determination of what the people want is a usurpation of popular sovereignty.

The majoritarian democracy that Rousseau envisioned is based on equality. Political conditions must be the same for all. All citizens must carry the same weight. There should be literally "one-man-one-vote." Partly to ensure that objective, society must not be made up of a multiplicity of groups and associations and have many centers and levels of power. Such a state of affairs distracts the citizens from what should be their exclusive concern, the *general* interest. To express its will, the people must form an undifferentiated mass of individuals. It is imperative that "there should be no partial society [*société partielle*] in the state." Subdivisions in the state were for Rousseau partisan interests that dilute the sovereignty of the people and

divert the citizens from the common good: "Nothing is more dangerous than the influence of private interests on public affairs." The
common good has nothing to do with taking into account the special
needs and aims of groups, localities, or regions. For the virtuous
general will to manifest itself, each person must decide freely and
autonomously for himself—"make up his own mind"—which is impossible if partial societies affect his thinking.[7] Social ties other than
those constituting the collective whole of the state divide the loyalty
of the citizens and block the formation of the general will. Rousseau
was at the same time a radical individualist, who separated the individual from groups and other subdivisions, and a radical collectivist,
who made the undifferentiated whole of the state the sole context for
virtuous political striving.

Rousseau's wish to free the current majority from all restrictions,
to dissolve the people into a homogeneous mass, abolish decentralization, and remove representative institutions could not be in sharper
contrast to American traditions of constitutionalism, federalism, localism, and representation. He was working out the sociopolitical
ramifications of a view of human nature that clashes fundamentally
with that underlying American constitutional democracy.

The virtuous society that Rousseau desired bears no resemblance
to societies actually known in history. In the new society, citizens
will have stripped themselves of separate social identities. They will
form "a single body" with "a single will." "There are no entangled,
contradictory interests; the common good is clearly apparent everywhere."[8] For Rousseau, the general will pronounced by the majority
was the final political word. There is nothing above it to which the
minority could appeal. The general will is itself the ultimate standard
of political right. The minority is by definition wrong and should
recognize its error. Not only is the minority not deserving of any
protection, but if it persists in opposing the general will it must be
coerced into conformity. In Rousseau's famous words, "Whoever
refuses to obey the general will will be forced to do so by the entire
body. This means merely that he will be forced to be free."[9] There
are no grounds for accommodating different interests. Political opinion divides between right and wrong, and there is no reason why
wrong should be tolerated. Political right is univocal, and power must
be the monopoly of those in the right.[10]

Rousseauistic political morality inspired the French Jacobins, who called themselves *les vertueux*, "the virtuous." They considered themselves agents of the people against vile conspiratorial forces. As the putative instrument of a new popular will in the making, Rousseau's fervent disciple Robespierre felt justified in crushing all opposition. Why should virtue not insist on total control? To the Jacobins fell the task of articulating the will of the people until the new social order had been established. The Jacobins set the pattern for all of those in subsequent political thought and practice who have turned against traditional society and thought themselves possessors of a superior insight and mission, giving them a right to dictate to others.

There are elements in Rousseau's thinking that sometimes moderate his extremism, elements that are compatible with a rather different view of man and society, but the preponderant trend of his thought and the one that has exercised the greatest political influence has been described as follows by the famous French literary scholar Gustave Lanson: His work "exasperates and inspires revolt and fires enthusiasm and irritates hatreds; it is the mother of violence, the source of all that is uncompromising, it launches the simple souls who give themselves up to its strange virtue upon the desperate quest of the absolute."[11]

Rousseau's notion of virtuous power has important implications for international politics. He can be seen as one of the founders of modern nationalism. The general will is the will of a particular people and can tolerate no opposition. Since there can be no appeal to an authority beyond the general will, conflict between states is likely. Rousseau pointed out that "all the peoples have a kind of centrifugal force, by which they continually act one against the other and tend to expand at the expense of their neighbors."[12] The weak may be swallowed up by the strong. Rousseau's thought had a marked militaristic bias. In the ancient Greek world his model was Sparta, as he imagined it: a spontaneously virtuous, unadorned, and unified society. For Rousseau, the nationalistic impulse was closely connected with virtue. "Do we wish men to be virtuous," he asked. "Then let us begin by making them love their country." "It is certain," he asserted, "that the greatest miracles of virtue have been produced by patriotism."[13] In his book on Poland, Rousseau advocated instilling an ardent nationalism in the citizens. "The newly born infant . . . must gaze upon the fatherland, and until his dying day should behold nothing else."[14] In the *Social Contract,* Rousseau wrote that the citizen should receive from the national collective "his life and being."[15]

Democratism as a doctrine of political morality thus receives its clearest and most uncompromising form in Rousseau. His notion of plebiscitary rule has held and continues to hold great appeal for champions of "the people," although these champions may, while waiting for the circumstances to become right for the desired kind of popular rule, behave in an emphatically non-plebiscitary, elitist way and may consider themselves forced by practical necessity to compromise the ideal. It should be clear from this examination of Rousseauistic democratism that emphasizing virtue as necessary for the good society is by no means a monopoly of ancient Greek or Christian political thinkers. Following Rousseau, the Jacobins gave great prominence to the need for virtue, only they radically redefined it relative to the earlier classical and Christian understanding.

Notes

1.   Jean-Jacques Rousseau, Social Contract, bk. I, ch. I, 141.
2.   Ibid., bk. IV, ch. I, 203.
3.   On the role of Rousseau in effecting a transformation of the imagination and moral sensibility of Western man, see Claes G. Ryn, "Imaginative Origins of Modernity: Life as Daydream and Nightmare," *Humanitas*, Vol X, No. 2 (1997).
4.   For further substantiation of the following interpretation of Rousseau's ethical and political ideas, see the analysis and critical assessment of Rousseau in Ryn, *Democracy*, esp. chs. V-VIII. For a general interpretation of Rousseau and his influence, especially on Western poetry, fiction and moral sensibility see Irving Babbitt's pioneering and brilliantly perceptive *Rousseau and Romanticism* (New Brunswick, NJ: Transaction Publishers, 1991).
5.   Rousseau, *Social Contract,* bk. III, ch. 11, 194, bk. I, ch. VII, 149.
6.   Ibid., bk. II, ch. I, 153.
7.   Ibid., bk. II, ch. III, 156; bk. III, ch. IV, 179; bk.II, ch. III, 156.
8.   Ibid., bk. IV, ch. I, 203.
9.   Ibid., Bk, I, ch. VII, 150.
10. On Rousseauistic virtue as demanding uniformity, see Carol Blum, *Jean-Jacques Rousseau and the Republic of Virtue* (Ithaca, NY: Cornell University Press, 1986). See also Ryn, *Democracy,* esp. part three.
11. Gustave Lanson, *Annales de la Société Jean-Jacques Rousseau*, Vol. VIII, 30-31. Lanson died in 1937.
12. Rousseau, *Social Contract,* bk. II, ch. 9, 168.
13. Jean-Jacques Rousseau, A *Discourse on Political Economy* in *The Social Contract and Discourses* (New York: E.P. Dutton & Co., 1950), 301-302.
14. Jean-Jacques Rousseau, *The Government of Poland* (New York: Bobbs-Merrill, 1972), 19.
15. Rousseau, *Social Contract,* bk. II, ch. VII, 163.

8

Love of One's Own and Love of the Common

"Your true republican is a man who imbibed love of the fatherland."
                                                            —Jean-Jacques Rousseau[1]

In preparation for later discussion of the neo-Jacobin view of international affairs and foreign policy it is appropriate to extend the dichotomy between two sharply opposed forms of popular government to two very different ideas of nationhood. A distinction is needed between what may be called patriotism and nationalism. Selecting terms for particular meanings is always to some extent arbitrary. "Patriotism" and "nationalism" have no universally accepted definitions. The proposed distinction may thus employ the terms in ways at variance with how they have been used by others.

The old morality of modesty and self-discipline, which has been seen here to be integral to constitutional democracy, does not preclude pride in personal strengths and accomplishments. Neither does it preclude local, regional, and national pride. Proper self-regard goes together with humility and appreciation for the attainments of others. Similarly, a proper patriotic celebration of national achievements does not signify a posture of superiority over all other societies or involve arrogance in the treatment of other peoples. Neither does it assume that there are no standards of goodness, truth, or beauty beyond national likes or dislikes. On the contrary, for the patriot, the standard for national self-regard is the same as the one that that may judge the flaws of his own people severely. The patriot is the first to feel shame and regret about unjust actions taken by his own country. Patriotism recognizes that right is not defined by national prejudice and passion. It maintains moral discrimination and self-control. The patriot, though always ready to defend his own country against threats, is less prone to impose his will on other nations than to try to set an example for them. Just as in domestic politics the constitutional democrat is not oblivious of the possibly legitimate claims of other groups, so in international politics the patriot is not insensitive to the interests of other countries. Indeed, as one looking to improve the quality of life in his own country, the patriot is receptive to the merits of other peoples and cultures and welcomes the variety of national customs as enriching the larger whole and adding spice to life.

Patriotism and cosmopolitanism, rightly understood, are compatible and complementary. The true cosmopolitan is not some culturally homeless free floater belonging nowhere in particular. He is just the opposite. It is because he has identified with and entered deeply into the finest achievements of his own people that he has learned to appreciate life at the highest level and become able to recognize corresponding strengths in other peoples. Like the patriot, the cosmopolitan is rooted in a particular cultural tradition but is to some extent at home in more than one country by virtue of the element of universality in his own particular background. Especially the more educated and cultured members of a civilized people are to some extent cosmopolitan to begin with. Russians are somewhat familiar with Italian music and painting, Americans with German philosophy, Englishmen with French cooking, Swedes with Anglo-Saxon political thinking, Chinese with Western technology and medicine, Pakistanis with Christianity, and so on. The cosmopolitan and the patriot both recognize that many peoples have contributed to civilization and that the highest values of human life can be realized in somewhat different ways depending on time and place. An awareness of a common humanity and destiny keeps the patriot considerate of competitors. Just as he does not demonize his opponents, so does he not regard his own side as above criticism. Even in the middle of a war with its practical imperatives, the patriot tries to hold on to his humility. Rarely in a conflict is all right on one side, and the present enemy is a possible future friend and ally. Civilization tries in various ways to keep warring parties in mind of the fact that they are fellow human beings. The Geneva Convention is but one example of the effort to keep that awareness alive even in the most unfavorable and difficult circumstances.

Nationalism, by contrast, is an eruption of overweening ambition, a throwing off of individual and national self-control. Nationalism is self-absorbed and conceited, oblivious of the weaknesses of the country it champions. It is provincialism without the leaven of cosmopolitan breadth, discretion, and critical detachment. Nationalism recognizes no authority higher than its own national passion. It imagines that it has a monopoly on right or has a mission superseding moral norms. The phrase "my country, right or wrong" sums up this attitude (though the person who originated it may have meant it differently). Nationalist politics is inherently intolerant, tyrannical, and expansionist. It bullies and creates ever-new enemies.

Especially when offered without appropriate definitions, the idea that democracies are inherently disinclined to aggression is conceited wishful thinking as well as historically questionable. All depends on whether a particular democracy has the self-restraint and wisdom that comes from character and civilized prejudices among its citizens and leaders. It makes a great deal of difference whether the democracy is of the constitutional or plebiscitary type. Plebiscitary rule aims to free the popular majority from checks on its prevailing will. In so doing it liberates also the desire for power and self-aggrandizement to which any people can sometimes be prone and to which nationalist demagogues can always appeal.

Rousseau can be seen as one of the founders of nationalism. His attack on traditional civilization was, among other things, an attack on the old cosmopolitanism of the West. With his idea of the general will as the ultimate standard of political good he simultaneously planted the notion that there is nothing above the will of a particular people to which other countries might appeal to try to restrain what they consider arbitrary and egotistical behavior. War becomes the only way to settle international disputes. In heeding Rousseau's general call for a new, virtuous society, the French Jacobins became pioneers for a special kind of nationalism, one that justified French expansionism by claiming that France, by virtue of its superior principles, was uniquely fitted to dominate and remake other countries. The Jacobins derived some pride and sense of superiority from their Frenchness, but the inner logic of Jacobin universalism is to shed specifically national characteristics and to become more abstractly ideological. The nation becomes an idea, the idea a nation. The nation becomes an instrument for universalist ambition. It is no longer something to cherish and defend for the sake of its unique culture. The American new Jacobins, though they do have some typically American traits, are attached to the United States less because they identify with the actual, historically evolved American nation with its ancient origins in the Western past than because they recognize the utility of the might of the United States and choose to regard this country as entitled to dominating and remaking the world because of its principles. Neo-Jacobin universalism has little relation to cosmopolitanism as previously defined. It does not have deep roots in a particular culturally distinctive nation. It arbitrarily invents a new moral and intellectual pedigree for America. In addition, it is neither humble nor prone to self-criticism. It is not inclined to respect the accomplishments and interests of other peoples. It wishes to impose upon other countries what it deems to be a virtuous order. In anticipation of a later argument, it might be added that many of the new Jacobins as well as many of their less ideological allies use high-sounding universalist language to dress up a strong will to power.

The world is wondering today whether in this century the most powerful nation on the globe will behave with humility and self-restraint or be an assertive, even bullying force. The influence of the new Jacobinism on American foreign policy, which will be discussed at length below, points in the latter direction. Indeed, the highly moralistic ideology and power seeking of the new Jacobinism indicate the likelihood of an era of international conflict and war. The neo-Jacobin quest for empire is bound to inflame international relations and generate opposition around the world—no matter that this push for control is undertaken for the sake of "democracy" and "virtue." Far from considering a subject of merely theoretical, academic interest, this book is examining an intellectual-political force that directly affects the future of the United States and the world. The nature and extent of the influence of the new Jacobins is an issue of great moment.

American discussion of the proper role of the United States in the world suffers from broad generalizations and false choices. Issues like trade, foreign aid, and military strategy are often said to pit proponents of a New World Order against persons who want to pull up the drawbridge around the United States. Those who have the greatest influence in the major media and in the two parties want the United

States to be internationally active in promoting free markets, democracy and human rights. The only alternative to this stance is supposed to be the view that the United States ought to play an insignificant role in the world and single-mindedly stress the national interest. Opponents of the New World Order are portrayed as isolationists and protectionists.

But this classification of views, besides being a simplistic rendition of the positions represented in the debate, ignores the possibility of a very different kind of foreign policy, one that simultaneously rejects globalist ambitions, be they ideological or more frankly imperialistic, *and* national self-absorption. This third possibility may be called responsible nationhood. It is possible for a powerful country, and any other country, to be guided by a patriotism that is indistinguishable from respect and fondness for diversity. A country can take an interest in other countries without assuming that they have everything to learn. Responsible nationhood can be defined in contrast with two equally questionable and often overlapping orientations: one an ideological universalism that wishes to replace religious, cultural, and regional identities with an allegedly virtuous homogeneity; the other a less ideological nationalism that is so full of itself that it has difficulty tolerating anything but itself. In practice, the two orientations become difficult to tell apart. Both undermine the possibility of peace with other countries. Responsible nationhood, by contrast, stands for a policy of self-restraint and respect for others in the international arena. It is cosmopolitan but not globalistic and threatening. It is patriotic but not closed-in upon itself.

Note

1.   Rousseau, *Poland*, 19.

9

Moral Universality: A Philosophical Interlude

"There cannot be natural right if the fundamental problem of political philosophy cannot be solved in a final manner."—Leo Strauss[1]

"The essence of philosophy is the abandonment of all authority in favor of individual human reason."—Allan Bloom[2]

The domestic and international aims of the new Jacobinism will eventually be discussed more fully in relation to the current state of Western democracy. Before doing so it is necessary to address in more general terms the problem of political morality. How moral universality is conceived bears directly on how one understands the present condition of democracy and the ideological posture and political ambition of the new Jacobinism.

In their championing of democracy, the new Jacobins claim to follow universal principles. They do not consider themselves mere partisans but represent verities that bind all human beings. These principles are impersonal and superior to all special and transitory human desires. They are for all times and places. They are the ultimate standard of right. This neo-Jacobin stance appeals to many conservatives who think that it resembles the old Western interest in higher values. The ancient Greeks believed that human life is subject to a universal standard of good that is either transcendent or embedded in "nature." Many Romans and Christians espoused notions of "natural law." Christians regarded the will of good as ultimately normative. The old Western tradition offered a number of variations on the same general theme of universality. Is, then, the new Jacobinism not simply reviving an older belief in higher values?

Some reflections on universality will throw more light on the contrast between different conceptions of popular rule and national conduct. Constitutional democracy and responsible nationhood assume moral restraint and discrimination on the part of a people and its leaders. With reference to what kind of standard is this self-discipline to be exercised?

Though the older Western tradition did not offer any single view of the nature of universality, the existence of universality was assumed, and the particulars of Western life took shape accordingly. The good, the true, and the beautiful, to use the language in which the ancient Greeks spoke of different aspects of universality, were for them not mere words expressing the subjective likes of individuals or the preferences of convention. These were the ultimate values of human existence. They were above and beyond the transitory tastes of time and place. They had an intrinsic, compelling power that could be progressively known by persons who undertook the protracted effort necessary to realize them in their own lives. The universal authority of these values became apparent in proportion as the individual let his practical conduct, thought, and imagination be informed and shaped by them. They were the source of "happiness" (*eudaimonia*), the profound, special satisfaction, distinct from mere pleasure, that comes with living as befits a truly human being. This form of human existence was the completion of life. The person who approximated it needed no further defense of its superiority. It was its own reward. Christianity placed a heavier emphasis than the Greeks on a happiness that transcends man's temporal existence, but Christianity, too, connected human moral and spiritual well-being in this world with a universal source of good. The Greeks, the Romans, and the Christians agreed that in politics might does not make right. Statesmen must struggle to resist pure partisanship in themselves and others and try to discern and act for the common good.

The older Western tradition in morality can be criticized on various grounds. One flaw is its tendency, under the influence of the more rationalistic dimensions of Greek thought, to intellectualize moral universality and turn it into a matter of right thinking. This tendency contradicts the emphasis, especially in Christianity, on the primacy of the need for *acting* as one should, the need for exerting the will to change the personality for the better. The crux of the moral-spiritual life, asserts the mainstream of the Christian tradition, is the quality of character. When Jesus of Nazareth said about himself that "I am the way, and the truth and the life," he was not setting himself up as the founder of a school of moral philosophy, inviting followers to think their way into heaven. He was encouraging will-action of a certain kind as the basic human need. Christians have stressed the fallenness of man and the importance of faith and divine grace but have also always assumed that true faith shows itself in concrete actions.[3]

But it is not the purpose here to go into the questionable tendency in earlier Western thought to conceive of universality in rationalistic and abstract ways. This tendency was for the most part superceded by other elements of thought and practice. The objective here is to show in general terms what the old Western tradition meant by universality. It is important to point out that Western universalism was not a doctrine about remaking man and the world. It held out the possibility of a better, more deeply satisfying human life, but the most important form of progress is moral and spiritual, involving a struggle with self and a recognition that man's weaknesses preclude more than limited improvement. The older Western notion of universality did not envision some kind of radical transformation of man's temporal existence (although Plato was attracted to such speculation). Society can become better over time through the efforts of its many individuals, but it is not possible to change the basic terms of human life. A spiritually and culturally richer and more comfortable existence can be attained, but if human beings do not successfully govern themselves at the center of their personalities, they will start using their economic and other resources in ways that undermine the kind of life that finally matters and even employ them for destructive, inhumane purposes.

The mainstream of the old Western tradition did not, in spite of the mentioned rationalistic tendency, understand universality in the abstract, separately from the concrete realities of human life as known in history. In considering how life might be improved it did not ignore given circumstances or treat tradition as irrelevant. Aristotle, for example, was interested in how good might be achieved in many very different political circumstances. All situations, even the most discouraging, can be improved in the sense of making them more conducive to the higher potentialities of human life. For a better society to be possible, moral and other higher aspirations have to be adjusted to what is concretely possible in the present. The standard for politics is for Aristotle not some abstract model hanging motionless above all particular societies in the splendid isolation of ideal perfection. Political morality does not mean conforming to a ready-made plan and shedding particularity for the sake of universality. Universality is a living spirit of good and can make itself felt in an infinite variety of ways, making use of any available circumstances.

Aristotle intimated that the historically evolved common sense of a people might be a guide to finding what was politically best for that people. In the natural law tradition, as represented, for example, by a Roman thinker like Cicero and a Christian thinker like Thomas Aquinas, a connection was made, however vaguely, between the ability to grasp the higher good for man and having at one's disposal the guidance of tradition. According to Aquinas, old custom and long-established law have a special dignity. Their very age suggests their being sanctioned by the needs of human nature itself.[4] Traditional patterns of life and thought would not have evolved, acquired authority, and become deeply entrenched in the first place, had they not been found by generations to answer reasonably well to the requirements of a good life. The natural law was not understood as something apprehended through the purely abstract ratiocination of particular individuals. It is a norm whose discernment requires the cooperation of many persons over time. Man is a social and political being who depends on others for the realization of his higher potentialities.

That there is a connection between long-standing tradition and universality can be understood less legalistically and rationalistically than has sometimes been the case within the Western natural law tradition. It is possible to conceive of universality more historically, in a way that, far from undermining universality, shows its infinite adaptability to, and, indeed, possible inherence in historical particularity itself. The historical sense is an awareness of the extent to which the past continues to stir in the present, of how history lies implicit in and affects current thought and action. Historical consciousness is also an acute sense of the specificity and uniqueness of historical moments. It is an apprehension of the simultaneous variability and continuity of human life.

The historical sense emerged in a thinker like Edmund Burke. Without saying so explicitly or with philosophical precision, he came close to understanding human good as the synthesis of universality and particularity. History contains much that militates against the good, the true, and the beautiful, and man's history is to a great extent the story of his selfishness, rashness, short-sightedness, violence, cruelty, and depravity. But where any of the three aspects of universality are present, it is in some particular form, that is to say, in historical shape. Goodness, truth, or beauty enter human experience only in the concrete.

The possibility of synthesis between universality and particularity was assumed in the Biblical declaration that the Word became flesh. Otherwise put, the Universal acquired individual historical form. The Incarnation is for Christianity a central idea, though its full philosophical import has been very slow to dawn on the Christian mind. Long only implicit in Western thought, the possibility of synthesis between the universal and the historical nevertheless exerted influence, and it eventually found more self-conscious expression in the philosophical idea that universality and historical particularity need not be incompatible, but do, on the contrary, positively need each other for universality to be realized in human life. The two are mutually implicated in each other wherever the good, the true and the beautiful are realized.

Another way of stating the same idea is to point out that universality is not an ahistorical, rigid, unchanging norm or set of principles. It is a living, infinitely adaptable potentiality that can enter into union with particular historical opportunities. Universality can make use of all situations, assume specific form according to the needs of personal and historical circumstance, although the obstacles to a better life are sometimes enormous and deeply discouraging. Diversity affected by universality is simultaneously unity in that such diversity builds up life of a certain moral, intellectual, and aesthetical quality. In spite of its endlessly different specific manifestations, universality points human beings in the same general direction—the life of the good, the true, and the beautiful.

Again, approximating the higher form of human existence is not the same as conforming to an abstract norm that defines ahead of time all that needs to be done. Achieving the good life in varying circumstances requires creativity. Sometimes individuals of superior insight and sensibility have to shake people out of traditional ways that have ceased to serve the higher life. Often the needed creativity takes society by surprise. Only after some considerable time does it become obvious that a particular convention had started to stand in the way of a fresh, richer apprehension of life's higher possibilities. For universal values to be expressed in a life that continually presents new challenges, individuals, communities, and societies must have freedom to find their own way. The same is true for entire civilizations, which means that the world as a whole should exhibit diversity as well as unity. The latter may be discernible only to relatively few individuals who can see beyond their own cultural sphere with understanding.

This is not the place to explore in depth the philosophically demanding question of the relationship between universality and particularity. Just enough has been said to set the stage for further exploration of the neo-Jacobin conception of universality and how it affects the view of society and the world.[5] The term universality can have drastically different meanings with drastically different practical ramifications. How universality is understood directly affects such all-important questions as whether to respect the traditions of a people, whether to make different countries conform to a single form of government, whether to permit a decentralized society and whether to be tolerant of deviating views.

Notes

1. Leo Strauss, *Natural Right and History* (Chicago: The University of Chicago Press, 1953), 35.
2. Bloom, *Closing*, 253.
3. For a discussion of the questionable utopian-intellectualistic tendency in Western thought that is strong in Plato, see Claes G. Ryn, "The Politics of Transcendence: The Pretentious Passivity of Platonic Idealism," *Humanitas*, Vol. XII, No. 2 (1999).
4. On Aquinas's view of the authority of custom, see the *Summa Theologica*, especially the section often called "Treatise on Law," Qu. 97.
5. On the compatibility of universality and particularity, see Claes G. Ryn, *A Common Human Ground: Universality and Particularity in a Multicultural World* (Columbia and London: University of Missouri Press, 2003) and Ryn, *Will, Imagination and Reason*, 2nd exp. ed. (New Brunswick, NJ: Transaction Publishers, 1997). For a discussion of the same philosophical issue with special reference to Edmund Burke, see Joseph Baldacchino, "The Value-Centered Historicism of Edmund Burke," *Modern Age*, Vol. 27, No. 2 (Spring, 1983).

10

Pluralistic Political Morality

"It is utterly on the basis of [the] general interest that society ought to be governed."
—*Jean-Jacques Rousseau[1]*

"You must entirely refashion a people whom you wish to make free, to destroy its prejudices, alter its habits, limit its necessities, root up its vices, purify its desires."
—*Maximilien Robespierre[2]*

"The recognition of universal principles . . . tends to prevent man from whole-heartedly identifying themselves with, or accepting, the social order that fate has allotted to them. It tends to alienate them from their place on the earth. It tends to make them strangers, and even strangers on the earth."—Leo Strauss[3]

The French Jacobins derived their philosophical method in part from the most rationalistic modes of thought in the older Western tradition, but they also took them in a radically ahistorical direction of their own. They introduced a new conception of universality, which, besides turning normative reality into an abstraction, departed sharply from the older tradition in substantive belief. The new Jacobins defined their own various stands in contradistinction to the moral, religious, and political traditions of the West. They summarized their ideology in the phrase, "liberty, equality, and fraternity." Their idea of political right centered upon equality. "The people" were to rule. Gone were the old notions, elaborated, for example, by Aristotle, that the proper political concern is for *good* government, not how many participate in ruling, and that different forms of government are suited to different circumstances. The Jacobins saw a particular social and political order as appropriate to all times and places and assumed that this order was sharply opposed to the inherited society

89

in which they were living. From the beginning, their intensely moralistic advocacy of a new society had a strong utopian cast.

Among those today who profess a belief in universality, it is common to understand the standard of right as a set of principles or precepts, discernible by reason, that announces its content apart from history and particular circumstances. The latter are considered irrelevant to ascertaining what is "simply right." In this perspective, political morality becomes conformity to a plan. This way of thinking is not exclusive to the new Jacobins, but they have shaped it to fit their own ideological and other purposes. Others who have fairly different substantive beliefs but are prone to similar intellectual habits—notably proponents of a rationalistic conception of natural law—have shown themselves susceptible to neo-Jacobin ideology and political direction.

The idea of political right as involving the implementation of a blueprint of some sort is difficult to reconcile with popular government of the constitutional type, as it exists, for example, in the United States. Many features of constitutional democracy, some of which it may share with other forms of government, suggest that this form of government is not an attempt to implement a static, preconceived moral plan. Government by popular consent, a willingness to accommodate different interests, decentralization of authority, adjustment to circumstances, acceptance of diversity—these indicate that a form of moral universality that is compatible with constitutional democracy must be historically adaptable and evolving, which is an emphatically non-Jacobin notion. In this more historical conception, morality is indeed universal, but it does not exist in the form of precepts that can be ascertained and articulated by the intellect once and for all. Universality is an imperative felt by the individual in the midst of a life that is only partially transparent, in which circumstances are never wholly known, and in which the consequences of action can never be predicted with certainty. Life is simply too large and complex for morality to be locked up in formulas. Even the wisest, most knowledgeable, and experienced individuals are very far from omniscient and they are, in addition, morally flawed. Their passions of the moment threaten to cloud or overpower their moral conscience. To say that universality has an enduring purpose is not the same as saying that its commands are clear and definite and that they produce a static moral uniformity. Given the changing and varying circumstances of political and other life, the moral imperative must be creatively and diversely articulated. Acting morally is never a matter of simply following rules, however helpful rules can sometimes be in steering the individual. If doing what is politically right were actually the same as following a fixed set of principles, as is the belief of the new Jacobinism, right would be strangely ill-adjusted to a political life that must forever address new, difficult, and sometimes wholly unanticipated situations and that always involves the special circumstances of very different people in a myriad of different places. No single individual or group can have the final word on what the common good requires.

A non-Jacobin statesman can rely on no moral blueprint for the good society. Neither can he follow one for conduct in international affairs. Even the most morally sensitive and responsible person is rarely certain beyond a doubt of what, specifically, is right in particular situations. It is ordinarily much easier to identify what in self and others is blatantly self-serving and clearly incompatible with the common good. An important objective of constitutional government is to hold back the more egregiously egotistical desires and to give at least a chance to those who are genuinely trying to discern what is in the common good. It should be noted, however, that intentions that are not censured as flagrantly partisan are provisionally judged to be not obviously incompatible with the general good of society and are allowed to pass into action. Concrete and specific aims are thereby enacted. To become a real power in human life, morality must be thus embodied in historical actions, and these must be adjusted to the special needs of circumstance. The universal must be realized through the particular. Together and over time, morally permissible actions give substance to and build up a certain quality of human existence. This purposive structure is a tentative embodiment of the good life, although one forever subject to reassessment and revision by morally alert human beings. Through a process of censure and qualified approval of particular intentions, moral civilization gradually evolves. Progress is neither automatic nor inevitable; moral decline and even disaster always threaten. Such advance as lies within human capacity depends entirely on whether those who live at a particular time will shoulder or shirk their individual moral responsibility and respect or ignore historical experience.

This historical understanding of universality assigns a greater role to self-restraint and humility than to trying to discern beyond a doubt just what is morally right in a particular situation. Human life is simply too varied, manifold, and enigmatic for there to be, except in rare situations, definitive clarity about how to act. Yet the new Jacobins claim to know what is "simply right," not just in a particular place or situation but everywhere and at all times. Their universalism assumes the existence of clear guidelines for how societies should organize and govern themselves. Those who question or oppose their moral-intellectual convictions seem to them perverse obstructionists, who may deserve ostracism, imprisonment, or even death.

The historically rooted sense of the universal that is indistinguishable from intellectual humility makes a person reluctant simply to impose his will on others. Sometimes exceptional individuals see further and more deeply than the rest of humanity, but no person or group, however enlightened and noble, can encompass and specify the needs of an entire society. Because of the sheer complexity and breadth of human life, moral good must be advanced in a multiplicity of ways. Most human beings have some potential for contributing in their own way to the continuing articulation of moral good.

Universality, it should be reiterated, is not the same as uniformity. Many different interests have legitimate claims and need to be accommodated by a society concerned about the common good. The universal does not abolish diversity. It harmonizes diversity. Moral universality blends with the uniqueness of countless personalities and causes, purging them of merely egotistical desires and letting them enrich the larger whole of society. Universality enlists them in its own cause by censuring whatever is merely idiosyncratic and destructive of moral community.

The phrase *e pluribus unum,* which sums up the achievement and the hope of the American Framers, does not signify the obliteration of diversity for the sake of unity. It signifies the harmonization of many different interests through proper self-restraint, both individual and institutional. The general good is not manifested in a univocal or homogenous way, as the Jacobins prefer to believe. Many groups and individuals will contribute to it in their diverse capacities and personalities, without giving up their distinctiveness.

The common good is also not the complete and final triumph of political right over evil. Men being what they are, they usually have mixed motives, and such moral harmony as is possible has to be realized in never-ending struggle with all that threatens its existence. The freedom that is necessary if individuals of conscience are to find their own course is available also to people of ignoble motives.

The thinking of the American Framers on this subject, explicit and implicit, is akin to that of Aristotle. The Greek was a strong advocate of politics serving the common good, but he also strongly resisted the idea that realizing this goal means simply superceding separate interests. The good society would not result from the imposition of virtuous unity, at the expense of social diversity. Partly in criticism of Plato, Aristotle wrote, "Obviously a state which becomes progressively more and more a unity will cease to be a state at all . . . . [T]he farther it moves away from plurality towards unity, the less a state it becomes . . . . The state consists not merely of a plurality of men, but of different *kinds* of men." Man is a social being; to become more fully human he must be able to receive from others the diverse benefits of upbringing, education, economic well-being, protection, etc. that he cannot supply for himself. Aristotle defended a kind of pluralism, though one very different from the kind of modern liberal pluralism that denies the existence of moral universality and recognizes only subjective individual preferences. Aristotle did affirm a moral standard above such individual likes and dislikes, but he believed nevertheless that it is a harmony of many different interests that will constitute a good state. It would be a mistake, he argued, to follow Plato's suggestion to try to unify the state as if it were a single individual whose soul should be ordered according to the principle of justice. This kind of unification from above which disdains particular interests would rob society of its reason for being, which is to put a wide variety of human roles and gifts at the disposal of the citizens, enabling them to grow as human beings. "So even if it were possible to make such a unification, it ought not to be done; it will destroy the state."[4]

As an ancient Greek, even Aristotle has an insufficient grasp of the importance of individual personal freedom to the moral and cultural welfare of society, but his critique, on moral grounds, of the desire to eradicate particular interests helps explain the nature of the totalitarian temptation, which so often lurks behind calls for "virtu-ous" politics. Real political unity, as distinguished from regimenta-tion, is indistinguishable from the kind of diversity that makes for a fuller, richer life. Precisely because constitutional democracy cher-ishes diversity and decentralization of authority, it stands in special need of the moral self-control and discrimination that will make plu-ralism and freedom civilizing forces and keep them from deteriorat-ing into factional conflict. Particularity and universality need each other, both in politics and in private life.

The pluralistic notion of moral universality that has been put forth here collides head-on with the Rousseauistic idea that virtuous poli-tics abjures particular interests and social subdivisions. In Rousseau's majoritarian democracy all right is found on one side, and only wrong is found on the other. Hence there is no reason to tolerate political diversity and opposition.

To sum up this discussion of universality and particularity, the notion that morality has nothing to do with respecting particular in-terests, particular circumstances, or historical precedent leads to deep suspicion of, or hostility to, the decentralized and pluralistic society and tradition-based ways of life. This willingness to disregard the concrete world in setting goals for society is a prominent feature of the new Jacobinism. Its abstractionist universalism excludes the pos-sibility formulated here—that universality may become a vital force in human life by finding expression in historical particularity and change. The implications of denying the possibility of a union of universality and particularity are stark and highly problematic. If political right is indeed adherence to a moral plan, personal freedom, social and political pluralism, decentralization, and even constitu-tionalism are, in the end, irrelevant to discerning and pursuing the common good. They will be tolerated, if at all, only as prescribed by the plan. No substantial room need be left for improvisation and new discoveries. The common good would be best served if those who know what is politically right were in a position to dictate to all other people, which would minimize the incidence of distractions from virtue.

Notes

1. Rousseau, *Social Contract*, 153.
2. Quoted in Robert Nisbet, *Conservatism* (Minneapolis: University of Minnesota Press, 1986), 10.
3. Strauss, *Natural Right*, 14.
4. Aristotle, *Politics* (Harmondsworth: Penguin Books, 1992) 104 (1261a15-1261a25).

11

Democracy in Peril

"America won't be good locally if it isn't great nationally."—William Kristol and
David Brooks

It should be evident by now that the philosophical issues just discussed have a direct and concrete bearing on understanding the state of modern Western society and the influence exerted by the new Jacobinism. It is time to turn in more detail to the problems facing democracy. The scope and seriousness of those problems could be illustrated by a very long list of examples. Only a few of them will be highlighted here that seem particularly indicative of Western society's simultaneous slide into factionalism, democratism, and conformity. Most of the examples will be taken from the world's leading democracy, but the phenomena cited have counterparts all over the Western world.

The gradual disappearance from Western society of the type of moral self-control and discrimination on which constitutional democracy depends has produced general sociopolitical fragmentation and an increasingly egregious pursuit of self-interest. The law, once regarded as an attempt to transcend mere power politics, is perceived more and more by lawmakers and voters alike as an instrument of partisan ambition, as a way of compelling the obedience of others, or as an obstacle to be removed. How the Constitution of the United States itself is widely viewed today is a prominent case in point.

A general decline of moral and cultural standards, accompanied by intensifying plebiscitary pressures, has gradually robbed American representative and other institutions of their aristocratic, restraining, deliberative function and made the electorate less accepting of that type of leadership. Since 1913 the U.S. Senate has been elected by direct popular vote, and, despite the six-year term of its members, it has become, like other representative institutions, very sensitive to the opinions of the mass media and the general public. The selection of the president by the Electoral College is nowadays a formality, though in the 2000 presidential election the purely numerical aspect of the institution affected the outcome. Today's candidates for the presidency are as subject to the vagaries of popular opinion and mass communication as are other candidates for office. The intent of the Framers has been largely subverted.

With the deterioration of the institutional supports for critical detachment and deliberation, responsible decision-making has become increasingly difficult. Among elected officials thought of the next election and the concomitant need to raise money is pervasive. In political debate most statements are made with a view to some political advantage. Rare is the politician who would risk unpopularity or media censure by stating uncomfortable truths. Successful politicians tend to be individuals lacking in deeper knowledge and insight. They are "pragmatists" without well-considered convictions of their own who are willing to go with the flow. Prominent figures such as America's Bill Clinton and Britain's Tony Blair are examples of politicians of technocratic-managerial disposition who are driven far less by an intellectually and historically grounded vision for their society than by personal ambition and political convenience, though, needless to say, they espouse the kind of concern for the downtrodden, at home and abroad, that has become synonymous with moral virtue and that is conducive to more power for themselves.

The typical national politician is harried and scarcely has time to read and reflect. He depends for information and opinion on snippets of news, media pundits, and summaries provided by staff. Instead of maintaining a critical distance from the political and intellectual fads of the day, this politician is swept up in them. His views and reactions to events are not likely to surprise anyone. Rhetorical posturing and electioneering squeeze out genuine deliberation and debate. The need to appeal to the great mass of people on virtually all issues pushes political discussion to ever lower levels of sloganeering and pandering. Elections become embarrassing displays of simplistic demagoguery in which advertising and media consultants play central roles. Judged by the appeals made to voters, the public is assumed to have a simplistic, even infantile view of their society and the world.

Although constitutional and other legal restraints have a formal existence still and even a fragile substantive efficacy, popular government is being eroded by plebiscitary, majoritarian pressure politics, a trend that is both generated and exploited by politicians and political intellectuals who think that it will expand their own power. The people are said to demand a more democratic society and a more responsive government, but, in practice, plebiscitarianism produces political passivity among the masses. Under the influence of a steady drumbeat of opinion from the media, people rather predictably stay within the prescribed bounds of political expression. Power is gradually transferred to politicians and their counterparts in communication and entertainment. Many citizens are aware that they are being cynically manipulated, but they do not know how to resist, and many have come to accept this state of affairs as inevitable, as a way of life. "Politicians" are widely viewed with disgust but are returned to office anyway. The rare politicians or intellectuals who try to counteract the general trends by stepping outside of the consensus of "respectable" opinion are up against a powerful momentum and risk vicious attack from the entrenched powers-that-be.

Modern welfare state politics and a long series of Supreme Court decisions have sharply centralized American government and undermined state and local autonomy. The people vote in elections as before, but increasingly their sentiments are shaped and mobilized by people far away who can decide what issues are important and define the terms in which they should be discussed. Great power of this type has been accumulated at the national centers of government and communication. Subjects that are abstract and distant from the voters are pushed into the forefront and draw attention away from tasks that are near and concrete.

Centralization of power goes together with attitudes of inaction and self-indulgence among people at large. That this should be the case is explained by the earlier discussion of moral virtue. The practice of personal, up-close responsibility that manifests and shapes character also buttresses localism and a decentralized society. Conversely, abdication of this kind of responsibility in favor of "great causes" that require the resources of government ushers in a centralization of power. A listing of examples of declining personal initiative, self-direction, and self-restraint is at the same time a listing of what undermines decentralized social and political structures.

Lawlessness and permissiveness are everywhere. Crime and shadiness are epidemic. What was long considered the fundamental responsibility of government—protecting the lives, limbs, and property of the citizens—is carried out only erratically. In many areas government lacks the ability or will to control crime. Most crimes go unpunished. There is a general hesitancy about enforcing existing laws. Doubts about the moral culpability of criminals and a reluctance to punish blur the line between criminals and non-criminals. In his description of democracy's lack of moral structure and drift toward tyranny, Plato wrote, "Isn't there something rather charming about the good-temper of those who have been sentenced in court? You must have noticed that in a democracy men sentenced to death or exile stay on, none the less, and go about among their fellows."[1] In the United States, justice has become so wrapped up in legalistic formalism that the question of substantive guilt or innocence frequently appears secondary.

Falling standards and fading self-discipline are prominent in all aspects of social life. Drug abuse is rampant. Sexual promiscuity is so common as to be widely considered no longer aberrant behavior. It causes epidemics of venereal disease, including AIDS, whose spread is limited only by a fear of illness. Abortions are performed in staggering numbers as a form of birth control. The family has lost much of its stability and cohesion and plays a much-reduced role as transmitter of civilized values. Standards of personal behavior and deportment continue to fall. Old-fashioned honesty and integrity yield to greed and opportunism. Lawyers, who were once regarded as officers of the Court and expected to respect the impartiality and high dignity of the law, increasingly twist, evade, and manipulate the law for unscrupulous clients. Other professions show a similar disdain for traditional standards of conduct. There may be no more telling sign of moral collapse than the number of priests who live personal lives abhorrent to their church or who ruthlessly victimize minors under their supervision. Corporate malfeasance shows greed and dishonesty on a sometimes monumental scale. In many fields, carelessness pushes out good workmanship. In sports, grossly irresponsible or criminal personal behavior is routinely tolerated that would have terminated careers not long ago. Commercialism is more and more obtrusive, advertising more and more vulgar and salacious. Spending for consumption through excessive borrowing is the order of the day both for individuals and governments. The continual inflationary erosion of the currency, which in some periods halves its value in just a few years, shows the opportunism and cynicism of vote-buying politicians and the complicity of self-indulgent voters who want benefits from government without paying for them. In education, standards are low and falling. Ideological fads and nostrums and the teaching of utilitarian "skills" are replacing attention to the insights, achievements, and history of civilization.

At the same time, diversions from real problems and responsibilities are everywhere. Entertainment forms an increasingly prominent part of Western culture and plays a central role in breaking down lingering traditional tastes and inhibitions. In the arts, the incidence of the crude, the ugly, and the offensive illustrates a collapse of aesthetical as well as moral judgment. The churches try to avoid the subjects of individual sin, repentance, and character and offer a largely sentimental message of "love" and "compassion." Many of them play a central role in undermining traditional standards of personal conduct. Old distinctions between what is morally admirable and deplorable are seen as "moralistic," "intolerant" and "outdated." Behaviors are accepted or held up for emulation that once were considered abhorrent. Again, one of Plato's comments about democracy's self-destruction comes to mind: voices appear in the decadent society and individual soul that "call insolence good breeding, license liberty, and shamelessness courage."[2]

The evidence of decline in today's Western democracies could be balanced against more encouraging signs, such as advances in medicine and technology and the ability of the economy to provide a high standard of living, but these phenomena are only marginally related to sustaining the kind of moral and intellectual maturity on which civilization in general and constitutional democracy in particular ultimately depend. Greater wealth, better health, and more creature comforts could be means to the higher life of the good, the true, and the beautiful, which was regarded as the essence of civili zation since the ancient Greeks, but increasingly economic and physical well-being are being divorced from cultivating the human traits that, according to the older Western view, offer the only hope for enduring meaning and happiness. Today wealth and health form part of a flabby culture of self-indulgence in which transient thrills of consumption, entertainment, sports, and sex temporarily cover up listlessness and gnawing desperation.

It is beginning to dawn even on the most naïve and unsuspecting that with the decline of traditional moral integrity and other self-discipline even the productivity and orderliness of the economy are threatened. Yet, in a fashion typical of our era, those who dominate public debate call not for a revival of character but for more laws and regulations.

It is hard to avoid the conclusion that civilization is disintegrating, not at the periphery but at the moral core. That core is the higher striving of individuals who try to make the best of the moral, intellectual, and aesthetical opportunities of their own lives, thus contributing to the elevation of the common life. To the extent that society's members restrain their merely partisan, morally lazy egos and treat others as fellow human beings, social tension can be reduced and genuine community, as distinguished from boosterish, forced togetherness, becomes possible. Today moral conceit permits flight from down-to-earth, up-close problems and opportunities to sentimental, self-applauding moral posturing. While high-sounding and ambitious goals are professed, social conflict intensifies.

These observations regarding the deterioration of Western society are obviously not meant to imply that there was once in America or elsewhere constitutional regimes wherein irresponsibility, superficiality, vulgarity, and cynical power-seeking were virtually non-existent and wherein dutiful statesmen and citizens served the common good. The weaknesses of human nature are chronic. Yet just as one people can be more admirable than another in important respects, so can it lose an earlier excellence. Today's American society is losing its moral, intellectual, and cultural strength and cohesion. More and more, its political and social life exhibits the characteristics of civil war by non-violent means. A spreading and deepening suspicion of the motives of others is well founded in experience.

Politics always has an element of raw conflict. In all societies order is derived in part from the threat of violence and other sanctions available to constituted authority. Another source of order is the enlightened self-interest of competing individuals and groups, which leads them to recognize the utility of limiting their assertiveness. Constitutional democracy, too, must rely on these sources of political cohesion. But more than any other form of government it also needs a special self-control and higher striving beyond the clever, calculating self-restraint of sophisticated egotism. In this respect, constitutional democracy is more difficult to maintain than any other form of government. It cannot function well without considerable moral and general culture among its leaders and people. An erosion of character and of concern for the common good may not immediately destroy enlightened self-interest in every sense; for a time, even blatantly partisan groups will recognize the advantage of putting checks on their self-seeking. In a democratic system it is politically prudent, after all, to try to gain the widest possible acceptance. But partisanship unbounded by respect for what lies beyond private advantage eventually becomes ever more grasping and aggressive, and soon self-interest does not even recognize the advantage of being enlightened.[3]

Modern Western democracy displays two tendencies that might appear unrelated and even opposed to each other but which are actually different manifestations of one and the same deterioration of moral community. One is the already mentioned social fragmentation. This problem is sometimes analyzed in terms of value relativism, nihilism, liberal pluralism or multiculturalism. The second tendency is the enormous and continuing expansion and centralization of government and of the educational, business, and media establishments that are closely intertwined with government.

Superficially regarded, what has here been called social fragmentation might seem an example of the kind of decentralized and group-oriented sociopolitical dynamic that has been described as integral to constitutional democracy. Is not what is labeled "fragmentation" simply a result of rejecting an abstract, universalistic, homogenizing blueprint for the good society and letting particular groups and interests proliferate? This may indeed be the case to some limited extent, but the mentioned fragmentation is primarily a sign that universality of *every* kind is being abandoned. It is necessary to consider the all-important contrast between groups and interests that are disciplined and harmonized with reference to a common ethical center and groups and interests that are not. Social fragmentation results from the self-assertion of individuals and groups who recognize no substantial obligation beyond their own partisan causes and who are therefore approaching each other merely as competitors or even as belligerents. In the absence of respect for a good that transcends the individual or his group, social order becomes fragile; persons and groups without any sense of common higher purpose tear at the social fabric, making it necessary in the end for government to use force to keep the whole from breaking apart.

If human beings recognize no moral bond that ties them together despite their diversity and disagreements, not even a particular group can form a genuine community. It can be only an aggregate of ego-centered individual interests that happen superficially to coincide; the group itself is threatened by conflict and disintegration. The more numerous the self-seeking individuals and associations in a society, the greater that society's element of fragmentation. Groups that do achieve real community internally do so because their members transcend their own merely private interests. Groups composed of members of that kind are able to find a common ground with other similarly motivated groups and can share with them in the moral and cultural life of the larger society. Again, real moral universality does not abolish particularity. It expresses itself in diverse concrete shapes in response to the needs of circumstance. Groups and individuals who pursue their special aspirations while recognizing the legitimacy of other interests and while adjusting to what lies above pure partisanship are the particularized embodiments of universality, and they create movement towards the ethical center. Groups and individuals who thus form unity in diversity cooperate in building up a common good.

Even in the best of societies groups will range in moral quality from the praiseworthy to the deplorable. The civilized society seeks ways of encouraging the former and restricting the latter. It does so far less by government regulation and coercion than by means of the unofficial patterns of communally and historically derived social premiums and penalties through which civilization manifests and maintains itself. Constitutional and other legal structures also play an important role. Groups are everywhere prone to disregard the rightful claims of others, and their self-absorption can threaten social order. Because of the wide latitude that constitutional democracy grants groups and individuals to pursue their own interests, that form of government more than any other needs a citizenry capable of self-restraint and broad views. Some externally imposed limitations on freedom are always necessary, but if, for whatever reason, the self-imposed limitations of groups and individuals become widely and greatly weakened, the constitutional system itself is in jeopardy.

In today's Western democracies, partisanship divorced from considerations of the common good is rampant. The danger keeps growing that constitutional democracy will succumb to the two mentioned forces, which appear unrelated but are closely intertwined: the fragmenting of society and the expansion and centralization of government—the latter expanding partly to try to absorb and control warring groups.

Regarding the enormous growth of central power, Robert Nisbet demonstrated that the modern administrative state is both cause and consequence of the deterioration of the older decentralized and community-oriented Western society. Centralized bureaucracies have gathered unto themselves power taken from or yielded by regional, local, and private authority. Of the particular historical forces that have greatly aided the accumulation and centralization of government power Nisbet attaches much importance to military mobilization.[4] In wartime, government assumes a larger role in directing society; it requires more of society's resources; it restricts existing freedoms; it introduces elements of a command economy; it becomes generally more intrusive. At the end of the war these added powers and functions are rarely fully dismantled.

The general point may be illustrated by the American government's response to the attack on the World Trade Center and the Pentagon, though it did not amount to a full-scale war. The need to combat terrorism at home as well as abroad could be cited as a justification for substantially widening the authority of government and restricting traditional American liberties. Here the Neo-Jacobin impulse so common in American public discussion helped dispel reservations and inhibitions. Political and intellectual activists who already wanted the United States to mobilize for a great international ideological campaign greatly added to the impetus for expanded government.

There was a time when Americans passionately believed that "eternal vigilance is the price of liberty." Government had to be watched closely, and attempts by it to restrict freedom had to be resisted. After the terrorist attacks on the United States many Americans, and especially political intellectuals and activists prone to neo-Jacobin thinking, have seemed markedly willing to let the federal government limit or set aside American rights and liberties, such as habeas corpus, the Fourth Amendment protection against unlawful searches and seizures, and the Fifth Amendment requirement that no one be deprived of life, liberty, or property without due process of law. The following words by the *National Review* editor and commentator Jonah Goldberg expressed a now widespread attitude: "[D]uring war time the president, as commander in chief, can declare someone a 'threat to the country' and lock him up without trial. If that scares you, get over it." After conceding that "your rights are 'unalienable,' according to the Declaration of Independence, which means the government cannot take them away from you," Goldberg cynically continued, "The sound-bite cliche that criminals 'forfeit' their rights frames the issue improperly. Criminals don't 'give up' their rights. The state determines that their rights can be ignored."[5] John Ashcroft, the attorney general of the United States, severely scolded those who were concerned about a possible curtailment of American liberties: "Those who scare peace-loving people with phantoms of lost liberty . . . give ammunition to America's enemies."[6] Sentiments of this type gave another major boost to the growth and intrusiveness of government. It is a telling sign of the transformation of American political and intellectual life that such opinions often, as in the just-mentioned cases, emanate from people called "conservative."

There has been much talk in America in recent decades of the need for limiting government. This has been true even of prominent candidates for political office, including presidential candidates. Many of them have actually been elected, which has made some political observers speak of triumphs of "conservatism." But the drive towards bigger and more intrusive government has continued virtually as before. There has been no significant and lasting reversal of the trend. Ronald Reagan's rhetoric about limiting and reducing government could not conceal that the federal government continued to grow during his administration. For example, he had committed himself in his first presidential campaign to the dismantling of the U.S. Department of Education. In America, he pointed out, education is by long tradition a local and state matter. But his second secretary of education, William Bennett, who stayed in that office into the administration of George Bush, was not inclined to reduce the power that he had been given. As is rather typical of neoconservatives, Bennett did not want to reduce federal power but use it for purposes he deemed salutary, such as inculcating virtue and American principles. Bennett actually sought a much-*expanded* federal role in education. In early 1988 he began pushing for a 21 billion-dollar budget for his department in the coming fiscal year, fully 50 percent more than the Reagan administration had requested for the current year. Bennett proposed the education plan that eventually became "America 2000" after Lamar Alexander had succeeded him. Bennett wanted to set national standards of education, a goal that was pursued diligently by his assistant secretary, Chester Finn. The program of nationalization, initiated by a putative "conservative," helped disarm conservatives who were opposed to the U.S. Department of Education and created an opening for additional federal educational initiatives. Bennett's plan made it much easier for the Democrats to introduce the plan that they, barely changing the name, called "Goals 2000," an ambitious bid for further nationalization of education.

Those who openly defend the expansion of federal power have created the impression that the expansion and centralization of the state is some kind of fated historical development, an inevitability given the great "complexity" of modern society. In the perspective of this book, the growth of government can be seen as related rather to a profound change in the self-understanding and way of life of Western man. People may call for a reduction of government, consider themselves conservatives even, but show in their actual voting and other conduct that they do not quite mean it. They continue to cede personal and local authority. To a great extent, the dramatic growth of government manifests the disappearance of an older notion of personal character and responsibility and a related conception of society.

The kind of social and political cohesion that emerged under the influence of the old Western ethos evolved primarily from within the many members of society as they tried in their diverse roles and locations to act appropriately and with respect for others. An internally induced and decentralized moral striving created a form of diversified social unity. Today that kind of unity gradually is being replaced by an externally and politically imposed order.

The fragmentation of society and the centralization of power are different forms of the abandonment of the old notion of community through self-control and up-close personal striving. Both are examples of the partisan pursuit of power at the expense of competing interests. The burgeoning bureaucratic-administrative state replaces the relative autonomy and mutual accommodation of a wide variety of interests with centralized direction and coordination. Although government elites routinely claim to be above partisanship and often invoke moral principle, their high-sounding language virtually always sanctions an expansion of their own power.

Plato cites variety, movement, and color as attributes of democracy. Having adopted what he regards as a silly and destructive assumption—that all individuals and all preferences have equal claim to attention—democracy is tolerant. It lets individuals pursue their own favorite desires as they see fit. Demagogues try to gain their favor by pandering to and trying to anticipate their wishes. Just as democratic politicians cater to popular whim, so "democratic man" follows his own impulse of the moment, which makes for a life of considerable diversity. Plato writes about "democratic man":

> He lives from day to day, indulging the pleasure of the moment. One day it's wine, women and song; the next water to drink and a strict diet; one day it's hard physical training, the next indolence and careless ease, and then a period of philosophic study. Often he takes to politics and keeps jumping to his feet and saying or doing whatever comes into his head. Sometimes all his ambitions and efforts are military, sometimes they are all directed to success in business. There is no order or restraint in his life and he reckons his way of living is pleasant, free and happy . . . [7]

Plato's description of "democratic man" seems to capture well a conspicuous aspect of today's Western democracies, but his associating democracy with freedom and diversity is contradicted at the same time by another and increasingly prominent feature of Western societies, their element of conformity and thought-control. Through government, mass media, education, and entertainment a moral-po-litical-cultural orthodoxy is promulgated and enforced. It changes somewhat depending upon the fortunes of particular pressure groups but follows a general pattern: it delegitimizes and tries to forbid tra-ditional beliefs while endorsing ideas that contradict those same be-liefs. Violation of the tenets of the new orthodoxy is grounds for grave suspicions about the offender and cause for ostracism, or worse. Professions of liberal tolerance and free speech somehow do not interfere at all with the desire to enforce ideological assent. Is it not a sign of unlimited freedom of expression to be able to criticize all authoritarian, intolerant backward and anti-democratic ideas? "Tol-erance" means in practice *in*tolerance of those who still cling to tra-ditional beliefs.

It is not necessary for the purposes of this study to describe the tenets of this orthodoxy in their most recent form. Suffice it to say that they lie opposite the views that people keep to themselves or express only in whispered conversation while looking anxiously over their shoulder to see who might be listening. The vigilance and mor-alistic righteousness of those who watch over adherence to the pre-scribed orthodoxy and behaviors call to mind the ideological relent-lessness and prying of the French Jacobins. The new Jacobins are by no means the only group trying to compel adherence to their views; on university campuses especially they have strong competition from groups that are even more radical in trying to dismantle the old West-ern civilization. The new Jacobins even appear conservative when defending their own Jacobin democratism and Enlightenment ratio-nality against postmodernist attacks. Though neo-Jacobins and postmodernists disagree among themselves, their combined efforts put people who would defend the old West under intellectual, social and political duress. Alexis de Tocqueville came much closer than Plato to capturing the pressures within modern democracy to con-form when, in the first half of the nineteenth century, he warned about "soft" democratic despotism in America. The time may come, he wrote in *Democracy in America,* when a uniformity of thought and manners will descend upon the American people. It may prove all the more thoroughgoing because it will be imposed not so much by government as by the people themselves. Anxious to conform to common opinion, Americans will police themselves and frown upon dissent. Unlike older, non-democratic despotism, de Tocqueville wrote, the new despotism "would degrade men without tormenting them."[8] Perhaps it is more appropriate to say that today's democracy has invented a new form of torture—the excoriating and demonizing of people who think independently, no matter that they may also be thoughtful, learned, experienced, and well-intentioned.

Notes

1.   Plato, *Republic*, bk. XIII, 376 (558a).
2.   Ibid., bk. VIII, 380 (560e).
3.   On the relationship among morality, enlightened self-interest and constitutionalism, see Ryn, *Democracy,* esp. 20-26, 166-181.
4.   See, in particular, Nisbet, *Quest for Community*.
5.   Jonah Goldberg, *Washington Times*, June 18, 2002
6.   Quoted by James Bovard in *USA Today*, October 9, 2002.
7.   Plato, *Republic*, bk. VIII, 381 (561c-561e).
8.   Alexis de Tocqueville, *Democracy in America* (New Rochelle, NY: Arlington House, undated), fourth book, ch. VI, 336.

12

The New Jacobins and American Democracy

"To celebrate the American Founding is . . . to celebrate revolution."—Harry Jaffa[1]

"America is forever new."—Michael Novak[2]

"Creative destruction is our middle name, both within our own society and abroad."
—Michael Ledeen[3]

The United States and other Western democracies may seem to have a long way to go before becoming oppressive, but there are signs that with the fading of the old moral and political ethos of constitutionalism democratic despotism is not only making strides but turning less soft. Individuals and groups who champion democracy not only for their own society but for the world as well are becoming more ambitious, well-organized, and aggressive. They are seizing opportunities for power afforded by the present precarious state of democracy, specifically, the crumbling of older standards for admission to positions of influence, and by unsettling national or international events. These proponents of democracy appear to many Americans of more traditional views but with limited historical and intellectual education to be defenders of the old America and Western civilization. They do after all warn against postmodernism, multiculturalism, and "moral relativism" as threats to American unity. They contend that America needs an infusion of "moral values" and a return to its "Founding principles." That their interpretation of those values and principles makes them virtually indistinguishable from the French Jacobins is easily overlooked by people who are anxious for any kind of defense of America. It does not occur to most individuals to inquire into just what kind of America is being defended.

Neo-Jacobinism claims to represent timeless truths that should everywhere prevail. The notion that the United States should promote democracy is far from new. Woodrow Wilson wanted Americans to fight the First World War to "make the world safe for democracy." The new Jacobins are reinforcing, intensifying, and giving new definition to the democratist impulse and turning it into a broadbased intellectual and political movement. Even individuals who are not themselves neo-Jacobin ideologues fall into the habit of using democratist rhetoric and of going along with neo-Jacobin plans. Many leading politicians lack the intellectual discernment to understand what is happening and are manipulated into embracing the neo-Jacobin cause.

As the new Jacobins regard the truths of democratism as being in substantial, if not complete, agreement with the beliefs and practices of today's Western democracy, they confer upon it a new moral legitimacy. America seems to them especially admirable and therefore to have the main responsibility for advancing the democratist cause internationally. The new Jacobins view the diligent promotion of their own principles as the way to overcome social fragmentation. Replacing diversity with ideological unity appears to them and to unwitting sympathizers an appealing prospect. Even more important to most new Jacobins is that America should be assertive abroad in behalf of the same allegedly universal principles. They have been quite successful in attracting to their cause Americans who are less ideological but nationalistic. That Western democracy in general and America in particular are in a festering crisis and might have reason to give primary attention to problems at home is for them a wholly unpalatable notion. They would like to undertake a great moral mission beyond the borders of the United States while imposing on that country their own virtuous order. The moralistic language of democratism masks and buttresses strong political ambition.

Among those who advocate a virtuous and internationally ambitious democracy it is not uncommon to draw prestige to their political preferences by attributing them or some portion of them to historical figures or classical works of moral or intellectual stature. Often they invoke a very loosely defined "Western tradition," sometimes the Bible, and various great books, which they interpret as offering support for their cause. Even a thinker like Plato, an icon of classical Greek philosophy but a thinker who might appear to have little or nothing in common with modern democratism, is used by them to boost the reputation of neo-Jacobin ideology. Similarly exploited are the Framers of the U.S. Constitution. The new Jacobins portray them as enlightenment thinkers and as having been under the influence of other theorists, John Locke prominent among them, whose thought they explicate with emphasis on its secular, ahistorical, and egalitarian strains.

It should not be forgotten that many of the new Jacobins espouse particular ideas for opportunistic reasons. Some of them have been influenced by Leo Strauss, who taught that the insightful who want influence must often dissimulate and seem to hold beliefs that will advance their fortunes. But it would be beyond the scope of this study to pursue the intricacies of the interplay between views held publicly and secretly. It is necessary here to concentrate on what the new Jacobins publicly profess, which is what most directly affects public opinion, without ignoring the more or less subtle role of deception. The importance of the will to power behind neo-Jacobin ideology has already been stressed.

In America, where the Constitution and the Framers still enjoy a very favorable reputation in politics, journalism, and large parts of academia, one way of being subversive of the Western tradition without being perceived as such is to endorse both but to reinterpret what they represent. Neo-Jacobin thinkers, thus, seek to present the American "Founding" and the Constitution as expressing a desire for giving America and the Western world a fresh start. According to Allan Bloom, the American form of government recommends itself as the implementation of an ahistorical moral plan. "Our story," he writes in enthusiastic language, "is the majestic and triumphant march of freedom and equality."[4] Bloom interprets "the American project" as advancing essentially the same plan as the French Revolution. The theme that America originated in and continues to celebrate revolution connects a large number of political theorists to neo-Jacobin thinking.

To sustain this view of America, the new Jacobins like to cite Jefferson, though not the Jefferson who defended state sovereignty but the one who has always appealed to the American left: the believer in "the people," rights, and revolution. His belief that revolution is needed to prevent tyranny is well-known: "I hold it that a little rebellion, now and then, is a good thing, and as necessary in the political world as storms in the physical."[5] Jefferson had a view of human nature and politics quite different from that which shaped the writing of the U.S. Constitution, but the new Jacobins choose nevertheless to treat him as most representative of the American spirit. Because of Jefferson's part in authoring the Declaration of Independence, they put the most radical interpretation on that document, certain phrases of which they take out of philosophical and historical context and turn into the essence of the Declaration. A historically informed reading of the document cannot overlook its being in large measure a listing of concrete grievances directed against King and Parliament for violating the inherited rights of Englishmen. The Declaration can even be seen as *counter*revolutionary, as a protest in the name of a status quo ante. Far from rebelling against British tradition, most of the leading men of America positively identified with it. Long after the War of Independence, at the Virginia Ratification Convention, Patrick Henry used glowing language to extol America's origins in Great Britain. "We are descended from a people whose government was founded on liberty; our glorious forefathers of Great Britain made liberty the foundation of everything. That country is become a great, mighty, and splendid nation . . . . We drew the spirit of liberty from our British ancestors; by that spirit we have triumphed over every difficulty."[6]

But the new Jacobins are interested not so much in the actual historical origins of America as in turning America into a vehicle for their ideological cause. The view that America is a revolutionary power is propounded by professor Harry Jaffa, who insists that America's political and social institutions must be seen as constituting a sharp break with the Western past. Jaffa writes, "The Founders understood themselves to be revolutionaries, and to celebrate the American Founding is therefore to celebrate revolution." The American Revolution may appear mild "as compared with subsequent revolutions in France, Russia, China, Cuba, or elsewhere," but "it nonetheless embodied the greatest attempt at innovation that human history had recorded. It remains the most radical attempt to establish a regime of liberty that the world has yet seen." The guiding principle of the Founding, Jaffa asserts, was equality. "American constitutions—state and federal—that resulted from the . . . revolution had *no* monarchical or aristocratic elements. They were not merely radically republican, but were radically republican in a democratic sense."[7]

Considering the marked continuity between American society and government before and after the so-called "Revolution," the Anglophile predilections of leading Americans, and the many aristocratic or quasi-aristocratic features of American constitutions, this highly tendentious portrayal of the United States is suggestive of an intense ideological commitment and a willingness to disregard historical fact in order to create the right ideological pedigree for America. To view the United States as the product of a revolutionary tide sweeping away the old West and as being founded on the revolutionary idea of equality is, to say the least, philosophically and historically forced. This interpretation of America's origins and characteristics shows a strong desire to have America be something quite different from what its history made it.

Allan Bloom agrees that revolution and equality are of the essence of the American Founding. Rather than be suspicious of ideas connected with revolution and other radical rejection of the past, Americans should, Bloom contends, understand that a revolution like the French raised questions that are central to understanding and fully realizing American equality and freedom and to addressing remaining problematic issues, not least of which is religion. "The domesticated churches in America preserved the superstition of Christianity, overcoming of which was perhaps the key to liberating man."[8] Neo-Jacobins who claim the U.S. Constitution for their side would like to think that it is subversive of earlier, traditional beliefs. They isolate it from its historical and cultural setting and interpret it in the abstract as pure text. Into that text they read their own preferred meaning, giving America a new constitutional Founding sharply different from America's actual past. In this interpretation, those who shaped the Constitution were enlightened lawgivers far above the simple, unsophisticated views of other Americans, and they set America on a brand new course.

The notion that the Founding was derived from the ahistorical ratiocination of a few individuals and represented a radical break with the past is so emphatically and richly contradicted by the historical record that proof hardly seems necessary. The Federalist Papers, for instance, repeatedly cite historical experience and precedent in support of their various points and even criticize abstract theorizing disconnected from historical circumstances. It would be folly, declares Federalist Paper no. 6, to "disregard the uniform course of human events, and to set at defiance the accumulated experience of ages."[9]

To treat Christianity as not integral to the American Founding is either to assume that a person's general outlook on life need not affect his political views or willfully to ignore an abundance of historical evidence. Various conspicuous, salient facts of American history are anathema to those who want the Founding to be a revolutionary break with the past. Whether one likes Christianity or the forms of it that predominated in early America, it is historically inaccurate and philosophically strained to regard Christianity, or closely related religious views of a more deist cast, as somehow extraneous to the thinking behind the Constitution. From the Mayflower Compact forward, key American documents expressing fundamental beliefs stress man's relationship to and dependence on God. A movement like the Great Awakening testifies as late as the 1740s to the continuing appeal and vitality of religious faith. The period before the writing of the Constitution was one of growing religious tolerance and liberty, and within the States the desire for disestablishing religion was growing, but the doctrine of original sin was commonly taken for granted, and government was seen as necessary to control the misconduct of a fallen human race. The view of human nature and society that informed the writing of the Constitution and so much else in American life, was deeply influenced by a Christian mind-set and sensibility. This was the case even among Framers who were doctrinally deists rather than Christians or who were religiously latitudinarian, skeptical, or indifferent. Many of the delegates to the Constitutional Convention, including some of the most influential, were appreciably governed by Christian assumptions.[10] The Framers as a group stood with regard to their view of human nature and society, as well as in other respects, within an old Christian civilization that had been transplanted in American soil and acquired deep roots there. That civilization had permeated the mind, imagination, and will of Americans in general, including many who did not consider themselves believers. Within their personalities people carry with them from the past far more than what they consciously and explicitly profess.

By taking the Founding out of its historical and philosophical context and twisting it in the Jacobin direction, American principles can be presented as a rejection of the old Western world. As the Constitution continues to be widely revered in America, thinkers like Bloom and Jaffa do not openly attack it but show it to be what they would like it to be. In this respect they are different from Thomas Jefferson, who, inconsistent though he was, openly disdained the Constitution for its anti-majoritarian, elitist bias and strong prejudice against radical political change.

Edmund Burke, who was a sharp critic of the French Revolution but generally sympathetic to American political thinking, saw great arrogance and superficiality and a great potential for tyranny in the idea that society should be made to conform to an abstract plan. Simply to disregard particular circumstances and the guidance of slowly evolved tradition and to rely instead on the theoretical constructs of a particular group of ideologues was for Burke a threat to all civilization. Bloom, in contrast, applauds precisely that approach and attributes it to the Framers. For him, the appeal of America is that it is a "great stage" on which the theories of philosophers and their students have been acted out: "There are almost no accidents."

Bloom ascribes to the American Framers a wish, similar to Rousseau's, to phase out social diversity and particularity and to unify human beings in their common denominator. To recognize man's "natural rights," Bloom writes, is to have "a fundamental basis of unity and sameness." In America, he argues, people are asked "to give up 'their cultural individuality' and make themselves into that universal, abstract being who participates in natural rights." To be a real American is to have shed historically evolved religious and cultural identities, what Bloom disparages as "diversity and individuality of culture." [11]

In Bloom's account, the U.S. Framers are egalitarians and exponents of "majoritarianism." Like Rousseau, they are also opposed to a diversity of groups and interests. "For the Founders, minorities are in general bad things, mostly identical to factions, selfish groups who have no concern as such for the common good." Bloom's critique of social diversity and pluralism stems from his ideological abstractionism, which regards moral universality as inimical to respect for particularity. Like Rousseau, he associates political virtue with sameness. Bloom describes the moral basis of the "American project" as follows: "Class, race, religion, national origin or culture all disappear or become dim when bathed in the light of natural rights, which give men common interests and make them truly brothers."[12] Political and social unity have nothing to do with historically formed loves and allegiances but derive from adherence to ahistorical universal principles. In Bloom's strained and even frivolous interpretation of the American Framers, they become virtually indistinguishable from the French Jacobins with their passion for *liberté, égalité* and *fraternité.*

Bloom's best-selling book, *The Closing of the American Mind,* was widely read as a defense of traditional Western civilization, but any reasonably attentive reading shows that by "the American mind" he means an Enlightenment mind, one that has left the superstitions and injustices of old Europe behind. What Bloom does not like is that this mind is being challenged.

Bloom's understanding of American principles is typical of the democratist ideology that is replacing the old ethos of American constitutionalism. This new ideology shares essential features with the thought of Jean-Jacques Rousseau, the quintessential plebiscitarian. This is one of the reasons why it is fittingly called the new Jacobinism. The latter does not agree with contemporary Western democracy in all particulars, but neither does it, in spite of its praise for the American Founding, offer much support for constitutional democracy as understood in this book. That neo-Jacobin theorists often invoke Locke does not change much, for Locke was only one of many influences upon the Framers, and his political thinking is in important respects different from theirs. What the new Jacobins endorse, moreover, is a Locke that they interpret as not dissimilar to Rousseau. Louis Hartz pointed to the Locke in question when he wrote, "Locke has a hidden conformitarian germ to begin with, since natural law tells equal people equal things."[13] The ideas of Bloom and others like him have much less in common with the authors of the U.S. Constitution than with such figures as Thomas Paine and Thomas Jefferson, who had strong egalitarian and plebiscitary leanings and who were uncomfortable with the spirit of constitutionalism represented by the Framers.

What is often offered as a moral tonic for American democracy thus includes a Jacobin passion for equality and virtuous unity that is likely to add to the push for uniformity and central control. The new Jacobinism supplements the pressures to conform with a moral and ideological rigorism. The belief that political virtue is summed up in specific "principles" or "rights" and that these are best understood by a certain intellectual elite with special powers of discernment breeds not only arrogance in those who consider themselves in the know but intolerance of those who deviate from the presumed moral prescriptions. Why, indeed, should the complexity and messiness of society not yield to the direction of the virtuous?

The potential for tyranny in this moral abstractionism is apparent also in the attacks on historical thinking by its philosophical exponents. The new Jacobins reject the belief that human life is inescapably historical and that the pursuit of good must be adjusted to time and place. Such a view is, they assert, a threat to moral universality and rectitude. To think of moral universality as in any way affected by historical circumstance is, so it is asserted, to dissolve moral universality. A real moral standard must be set apart from the historical phenomena for which it is to be the standard. Besides revealing rather amateurish philosophical habits, this belief in the existence of a morally pure vantage point outside of history discloses the ground for denying any moral legitimacy to individuality, particularity, and diversity as such. Only the neo-Jacobin notion of right deserves respect.[14]

At a time of sociopolitical disintegration the new Jacobinism offers a vision of moral politics. Like the old Jacobins, the new Jacobins put great emphasis on the need for "virtue." It plants the idea that political right could be imposed from above by the insightful. Plato's notion in the *Republic* that an elite of philosophers should lead society may be the real reason for his attraction to the new Jacobins. Like Rousseau, they see politics as a choice between right and wrong. If power could be acquired by those who champion right, there is no reason, except pragmatic considerations, to respect or accommodate a diversity of views and interests. Unlike the old virtue of character, the new virtue does not aim primarily at controlling self but at controlling others.

One vehicle for the expansion of virtuous power that the new Jacobins favor is a vigorous presidency. Here the long-standing liberal-leftist glorification of the presidency as best suited to doing the people's will—a stance well exemplified by James MacGregor Burns, a former president of the American Political Science Association—blends with the notion of presidential leadership advocated by a neoconservative like Harvey Mansfield.[15]

To summarize this chapter, it is important to understand that, though neo-Jacobinism often presents itself to Americans as conservative of the so-called Founding, it regards that Founding as being itself a rejection of traditional Western society. According to this view, America is, by virtue of its principles, a quintessentially revolutionary force. Both at home and abroad it replaces traditional ways with a unitary and virtuous order. One writer who openly and explicitly celebrates America as a destroyer of inherited ways of life is Michael Ledeen, who was an advisor on national security in the Reagan White House. Ledeen says fondly of Americans and "America's mission": "Creative destruction is our middle name, both within our society and abroad. We tear down the old order every day, from business to science, literature, art, architecture, and cinema to politics and the law. Our enemies have always hated this whirlwind of energy and creativity, which menaces their traditions (whatever they may be) and shames them for their inability to keep pace . . . . [We] must destroy them to advance our historic mission."[16]

Democratism is not new and has no single source, but its definition and political influence today is due in large part to the ideological fervor and political energy of the new Jacobins. Their insistence that democracy is a great moral cause appeals to a number of constituencies: to conservatives who bemoan "value-relativism," to liberals who think the Welfare State could use a moral boost and a renewed sense of self-worth, to leftists who like the stress on equality, revolution, and starting over, and to nationalists, investors, and businessmen who welcome a moral justification for American assertiveness abroad. These groups may have far more in common than they think.

Notes

1. Jaffa, Equality as a Conservative Principle," 86.
2. Michael Novak, *Washington Times*, January 20, 1989.
3. Michael Ledeen, *The War Against the Terror Masters* (New York: St. Martin's Press, 2002) 212-13.
4. Bloom, *Closing*, 97.
5. Jefferson, Letter to John Taylor, May 28, 1816, *Life and Selected Writings*, 413.
6. Patrick Henry, Viriginia Ratification Convention, 1788.
7. Jaffa, "Equality as a Conservative Principle," 86.
8. Bloom, *Closing*, 161.
9. *Federalist*, 54.
10. For a discussion of the religious views of the framers, see René de Visme Williamson, *Independence and Involvement* (Baton Rouge: Louisiana State University Press, 1964), esp. pp. 213-24.
11. Bloom, *Closing*, 97, 30-32. For an extensive analysis and assessment of Bloom's book, see Claes G. Ryn, "Universality or Uniformity?" *Modern Age, Vol.* 32, No. 1 (1988).
12. Bloom, *Closing*, 31, 27. Bloom wants an exception to society's majoritarian regime in the universities, where the insightful should guide disciples toward enlightenment.
13. Louis Hartz, *The Liberal Tradition in America* (New York: Harcourt, Brace, Jovanovich, 1955), 11.
14. In the United States, much of the contemporary hostility to a philosophical concern for historical particularity is derived from Leo Strauss, who in turn relies on German sources. See, for example, Strauss, *Natural Right ,* esp. 294-323. For a critique of Strauss' anti-historicism, see Claes G. Ryn, "History and the Moral Order," in Francis Canavan, ed., *The Ethical Dimension of Political Life* (Durham, NC: Duke University Press, 1983), and Baldacchino, "Value Centered Historicism," which challenges Strauss' view of Burke. The anti-historicist brand of thinking is often simplistic and reductionistic. See, for example, Fred Baumann, "Historicism and the Constitution," in Allan Bloom, ed., *Confronting the Constitution* (Washington, DC: American Enterprise Institute, 1990). For a critique of the contemporary attacks on historical thinking, see Paul Gottfried, *The Search for Historical Meaning* (DeKalb: Northern Illinois University Press, 1986); and Ryn, *Will, Imagination and Reason*, which defends historical consciousness as not only compatible with but indispensable to a defense of ethical and other universality.
15. See James MacGregor Burns, *The Deadlock of Democracy* (Englewood Cliffs, NJ: Prentice-Hall, 1963) and Harvey Mansfield, *Taming the Prince* (New York: Free Press, 1989).
16. Ledeen, *Terror Masters,* 213.

13

Democracy for the World

"The United States should stand up and lead the world democracy movement. We have made democracy work here; now we ought to make it work everywhere we can, with whatever tough and expensive action that takes."—James David Barber[1]

"Supporting democracy is a vital American endeavor. It is nothing to be ashamed of and nothing to be stingy about."—Charles Krauthammer[2]

"Remember this about American Purpose: A unipolar world is fine, if America is the uni."—Ben Wattenberg[3]

"Liberalism is the only ideology with the right to citizenship in today's world." —Francis Fukuyama[4]

"The consciousness of having willed the welfare of his fellow men is the reward of the virtuous man. The gratitude of the multitude [surrounds] his memory with honors."—Maximilien Robespierre[5]

It is time to examine more closely the neo-Jacobin approach to foreign policy and international affairs. The most prominent and salient feature of this approach is its universalistic and monopolistic claims, which seem indistinguishable from an unrelenting will to power. Allan Bloom makes clear that what he calls "the American project" is not just for Americans: "When we Americans speak seriously about politics, we mean that our principles of freedom and equality and the rights based on them are rational and everywhere applicable." World War II was for Bloom not simply a struggle to defeat a dangerous enemy. It was "really an educational project undertaken to force those who did not accept these principles to do so."[6] If America is the instrument of universal right, the cause of all humanity, it is only proper that it should be diligent and insistent in imposing its will.

Bloom was a professor at the University of Chicago, but a large number of American intellectual activists, journalists, and columnists, many of them taught by professors of similar outlook, sound the same theme. The theme is so common in the major media, newspapers, and intellectual magazines and is so often echoed by politicians that it might be taken as expressing a self-evident truth. It has a markedly Jacobin ring.

Not all who speak about the United States having a global mission to spread democracy need be neo-Jacobins in a thoroughgoing sense. Some use neo-Jacobin rhetoric not out of ideological conviction, but because such language is in the air and appears somehow expected. Many combine Jacobin ideas with different elements of thought and imagination. As has been previously discussed, contradictory notions often compete within one and the same person. In this chapter as elsewhere it is not assumed that every individual who has expressed Jacobin sentiments should for that reason be classified as a Jacobin and nothing else. Though some of the individuals quoted in this book come close to being just that, the primary purpose is not to classify particular individuals but to identify a particular intellectual-political dynamic with its own inner logic, to show how certain ideas belong together and form a coherent, if philosophically highly questionable, ideology.

Before proceeding with the analysis of neo-Jacobin thinking in world affairs, a point previously made should be reiterated: To question the imperialistic ambitions of the neo-Jacobins is not the same as to question a prominent role for the United States in the world. America must defend itself, protect its interests, and shoulder some of the responsibility for the peace and well-being of the world. The United States and the Western world face huge challenges, including the possible intensification of tensions among the civilizations of the world. To act wisely in a world of great dangers as well as opportunities America does indeed need a strategy, one based on mature, historically well-informed, subtle thinking and marked by humility.[7] What is argued here is that the strategy of neo-Jacobinism does not answer to that description. It threatens to inflict great damage and suffering on both America and the world. It expresses moral and intellectual conceit and feeds an inordinate desire for power. If permitted to shape government policy, it is likely to multiply and aggravate the problems faced by the United States and the Western world, partly by inspiring American foreign policy conduct that fans the flames of anti-Western feeling.

Two writers with considerable media visibility, William Kristol and David Brooks, who label themselves conservatives, have complained that the old prejudice among American conservatives against big and growing American federal government is foolish. Big government is needed, Kristol and Brooks contend, because the United States is based on "universal principles." Its special moral status gives it a great mission in the world. To pursue its global task the American government must be muscular and "energetic," especially with regard to military power. What is needed, argue Kristol and Brooks, is a "national-greatness conservatism" that advocates "a neo-Reaganite foreign policy of national strength and moral assertiveness abroad."[8]

Parallels between this kind of advocacy and the thinking of the French Jacobins are ubiquitous in American political-intellectual and journalistic circles. Robert Kagan writes sympathetically of his fellow Americans, "As good children of the Enlightenment, Americans believe in human perfectibility. But Americans also believe . . . that global security and a liberal order depend on the United States—that 'indispensable nation'—wielding power."[9]

International adventurism has often served to distract nations from pressing domestic difficulties, but in America today expansionism is often also fueled by intense moral-ideological passion. Since the principles for which America stands are portrayed as ultimately supranational—for Bloom they are actually opposed to traditional national identity—"nationalism" may be not quite the right term for this new missionary zeal. The new Jacobins believe that as America spearheads the cause of universal principles, it should progressively shed its own historical distinctiveness except in so far as that distinctiveness is directly related to those principles. Countries confronted by this power, on the other hand, are likely to see it as little more than a manifestation of nationalistic ambition and arrogance, but it is nationalistic only in a special sense. Like revolutionary France, neo-Jacobin America casts itself as a Savior Nation. Ideological and national zeal become indistinguishable. "Our nationalism," write Kristol and Brooks about America's world wide mission, "is that of an exceptional nation founded on a universal principle, on what Lincoln called 'an abstract truth, applicable to all men and all times.'"[10]

This view of America's role cannot be called patriotic under the definition proposed above. It is not characterized by devotion to America's concrete historical identity with its origins in Greek, Roman, Christian, European and English civilization. Neo-Jacobins are attached in the end to ahistorical, supranational principles that ought to replace the traditions of particular societies. Also, humility is not a notable part of the neo-Jacobin make-up. Neo-Jacobins sees themselves as on the side of right fighting evil. Neither are the neo-Jacobins prone to respect or look for common ground with countries that do not share their preference for democracy. If they tolerate the governments of these societies, it is only because these regimes cannot yet conveniently be transformed or because they are useful as allies against regimes that are deemed more acutely unacceptable.

As explained earlier, the patriot's pride of country is indistinguishable from moral self-restraint and a sense of the flaws of his own country. American neo-Jacobinism is perhaps best described as a kind of ideological nationalism. The new Jacobins are not precisely uncritical of today's American democracy; Bloom and others complain that it is too relativistic and insufficiently faithful to the principles of its own Founding. But it should be carefully noted that those principles are regarded as "rational and everywhere applicable" and thus as monopolistic. Greater dedication to "American principles" would by definition increase, not reduce, the wish of Americans to dictate terms to others.

Having been nurtured for many years in pockets of the academy, American neo-Jacobinism started to acquire journalistic and political critical mass in the 1980s. It was well represented in the national security and foreign policy councils of the Reagan and Bush, Sr. administrations. As Soviet communism was crumbling it seemed to people of this orientation increasingly realistic to expect an era in which the United States would be able to dominate the world in behalf of universal principles. Missionary zeal and the desire to use American power started to flood the media, government, and the public policy debate. The columnist and TV commentator Ben Wattenberg offered a particularly good example of this frame of mind. In 1988, he wrote that the prospects for exporting American values were highly propitious. "Never," he stated with pride and satisfaction, "has the culture of one nation been so far-flung and potent." He pointed out that "there is, at last, a global language, American."

After the Cold War the potential for the further spread of American culture was enormous, Wattenberg wrote. "Consider: last year alone, forty million VCRs were sold; the cassettes that go into them show mostly American movies and music. Important newsstands around the world now sell three American daily newspapers. There is now a near-global television news station: Cable News Network." Not mentioned by Wattenberg was that the content being transmitted to the world might be of dubious value and be regarded as a poor reflection on America and democracy among discriminating observers abroad, not just among anti-American radical ideologues. What intrigued him was the potential to expand American influence by exporting America's culture.

Behind the argument that the United States and its values are models for all peoples lurked the will to power, which was sometimes barely able to keep up ideological appearances. Again by way of example, Wattenberg desired nothing less than world dominance: "It's pretty clear what the global community needs: probably a top cop, but surely a powerful global organizer. Somebody's got to do it. We're the only ones who can." He called "visionary" the idea of "spreading democratic and American values around the world." With moralistic righteousness he added, "It's the right thing to do." As if not to appear immodest, Wattenberg wrote, "Our goal in the global game is not to *conquer* the world, only to *influence* it so that it is hospitable to our values."[11] Later he urged, "Remember this about American Purpose: A unipolar world is fine, if America is the uni."[12]

In the major media, one of the early and most persistent advocates of an assertive American foreign policy was the columnist and TV commentator Charles Krauthammer. In 1991, for example, he urged a "robust interventionism." "We are living in a unipolar world," he wrote. "We Americans should like it—and exploit it." "Where our cause is just and interests are threatened, we should act—even if . . . we must act unilaterally."[13] This point of view would eventually become a commonplace.

The idea of spreading democracy sometimes took on a religious ardor. In a Christmas column published in 1988, Michael Novak described this form of government as ordained by God. The Judaeo-Christian tradition "instructs the human race to make constant progress . . . . It insists that societies must continually be reshaped, until each meets the measure the Creator has in mind for a just, truthful, free, and creative civilization." All over the world people were "crying out against abuses of their God-given rights to self-determination." The spread of democracy was for Novak a great religious development. He compared it to God's Incarnation. The "citizens of the world . . . demand the birth of democracy in history, in physical institutions: as physical as the birth at Bethlehem."[14] The enthusiasm of the Christmas season may have inclined Novak to overstatement, but he was clearly eager to have his readers associate democracy with divine intent. It might be added that Novak's thinking has evolved and contains elements and potentialities that point away from an uncritical democratism.

The identification of Christianity with democracy was attempted with varying degrees of intensity and intellectual sophistication by a number of well-known individuals, ranging from Novak and Richard John Neuhaus to Margaret Thatcher. This mode of thinking is in marked contrast to the old Christian tradition. Christianity has always stressed the imperfect, sinful nature of man and warned against placing too much faith in man-made political institutions and measures. Augustine (354-430) is only one of the earliest and least sanguine of many Christian thinkers over the centuries who would have rejected out of hand the idea that mankind is destined for great progress and political perfection, to say nothing of the possibility of salvation through politics. Although Christianity has stressed that rulers must serve the common good and behave in a humane manner, it has been reluctant to endorse any particular form of government as suited to all peoples and all historical circumstances. Here Christianity agreed with the Aristotelian view.

Democratism has long had more than a foothold in American government. A look back in modern history is appropriate. President Woodrow Wilson with his belief in America's special role and his missionary zeal gave democratism a strong push. The Harvard professor Irving Babbitt (1865-1933), perhaps America's most incisive and prescient student of modern Western and American culture, commented in the early years of the twentieth century on the imperialistic trend in U.S. foreign policy. Babbitt, the founder of what has been called the New Humanism or American Humanism, was formally a professor of French and comparative literature, but he was also a

highly perceptive as well as prophetic observer of social and political developments. He noted that the United States was setting itself
up as the great guardian and beneficiary of mankind. "We are rap-
idly becoming a nation of humanitarian crusaders," Babbitt wrote in
1924. Leaders like Wilson viewed America as abjuring selfish motives and as being, therefore, above all other nations. Babbitt commented, again in 1924,

> We are willing to admit that all other nations are self-seeking, but as for ourselves, we
> hold that we act only on the most disinterested motives. We have not as yet set up, like
> revolutionary France, as the Christ of Nations, but during the late war we liked to look
> on ourselves as at least the Sir Galahad of Nations. If the American thus regards himself
> as an idealist at the same time that the foreigner looks on him as a dollar-chaser, the
> explanation may be due partly to the fact that the American judges himself by the way he
> feels, whereas the foreigner judges him by what he does.[15]

By the time of President Wilson the idea had long been common
in America that in old Europe conceited and callous elites oppressed
the common man. There and elsewhere things needed to be set right.
Thomas Jefferson had been a pioneer for this outlook. But from the
time of George Washington's warning of the danger of entangling
alliances, a desire for heavy American involvement abroad had for
the most part been held in check. By the time of Theodore Roosevelt's
presidency, it was clear that the wish for American prominence and
activism in international affairs had thrown off earlier restraints.
Woodrow Wilson reinforced the interventionist impulse, not, of
course, to advance selfish American national motives but, as he said,
to "serve mankind." Because America has a special moral status,
Wilson proclaimed, it is called to do good in the world. In 1914,
even before the outbreak of the European war, Wilson stated in a
Fourth of July address that America's role is to serve "the rights of
humanity." The flag of the United States, he declared, is "the flag,
not only of America, but of humanity."[16] It seemed to Wilson that
when the United States entered the First World War it became a war
to make the world safe for democracy. What America touched, it
blessed.

Babbitt pointed out that those who would not go along with Wilson's
"humanitarian crusading" were warned that they would "break the
heart of the world." Babbitt retorted, "If the tough old world had ever
had a heart in the Wilsonian sense, it would have been broken long

ago." He added that Wilson's rhetoric, which was at the same time abstract and sentimental, revealed "a temper at the opposite pole from that of the genuine statesman." Wilson's humanitarian idealism made him "inflexible and uncompromising."[17]

The notion that America has a mandate to help rid the world, not least Europe, of the bad old ways of traditional societies remained a strong influence on American foreign policy. In the Second World War, Franklin Roosevelt could find at least some limited common ground with Stalin beyond military objectives in that the latter was especially hostile to traditional societies ruled by old elites.

For a long time during the Cold War, most policymakers and commentators saw that war as a defensive struggle to protect freedom or liberty against totalitarian tyranny. But some of the most dedicated cold warriors were also democratists. They had a vision for remaking the world that differed in substance from that of the Soviet Union and other communist regimes but that was equally universalistic. With the disintegration and collapse of the Soviet Union, these cold warriors did not argue for substantially reducing the American military or the United States' involvement in international affairs. On the contrary, they believed that America should continue to play a large and, in some respects, expanded role in the world. As the only remaining superpower, America had a historic opportunity to advance the cause of democracy and human rights. This language had long been gaining currency in the centers of public debate and political power, and soon government officials and politicians in both of the major parties spoke routinely of the need to promote democracy. Many did so in just the manner here associated with neo-Jacobinism. It seemed to them that the American ideology had not only survived the challenge from the other universalist ideology, but had prevailed in a contest that validated the American ideal as applicable in all societies. One universalist ideology having been defeated, another wanted to enact its own vision for the world.

The first President Bush thought of himself as a competent pragmatist, but, as is often the case with persons who lack philosophically grounded convictions of their own, he was susceptible to adopting the language and ideas of intellectually more focused and ideological individuals. The rhetoric in his administration about a New World Order often had a distinctly democratist ring, in considerable part probably because of the ideological leanings of speechwriters. In 1991 James Baker, President Bush's secretary of state, echoed a neo-Jacobin refrain when he declared that U.S. foreign policy should serve not specifically American interests but "enlightenment ideals of universal applicability." Whether such formulations originated with Mr. Baker or his speechwriters, the secretary clearly liked the sound of them. Mr. Baker advocated "A Euro-Atlantic community that extends east from Vancouver to Vladivostok." This "community," he said, "can only be achieved on a democratic basis." The enormous size and enormous political and cultural diversity of the region he described did not give him pause or make him question the United States' willingness or ability to take charge of such a daunting cause. No, the United States should promote "common . . . universal values" in those parts of the world, he said, and "indeed, elsewhere on the globe."[18] American power was there to be used. It seems appropriate in cases such as these to talk of virtually unlimited political ambition.

The surge of globalist political-ideological aspirations was even more blatantly and pointedly expressed by the Bush, Sr. administration in a draft Pentagon planning document that was leaked to the *New York Times*. It had been produced under the supervision of then Undersecretary of Defense Paul Wolfowitz. The draft plan dealt with the military needs of the United States in the post-Cold War era, setting forth the goal of a world in which the United States would be the sole and uncontested superpower. Probably over the objections of some military leaders, the draft plan assigned to the United States "the pre-eminent responsibility" for dealing with "those wrongs which threaten not only our interests, but those of our allies or friends, or which could seriously unsettle international relations." The goal of American world dominance was presented as serving the spread of democracy and open economic systems. American military power was to be so overwhelming that it would not even occur to competitors of the United States to challenge its will.[19]

This vision of the future might have seemed the expression of an inordinate, open-ended, even megalomaniacal desire for power and control, uninhibited by the fact that the world is, after all, rather large. Significantly, many commentators considered the vision entirely plausible. Among those who were quick to express not reservations but great satisfaction with the draft plan was Charles Krauthammer, who strongly endorsed the idea of "deterring potential competitors from even aspiring to a larger regional and global role."[20] The *Wall Street Journal* praised the draft plan in a lead editorial favoring "Pax Americana."[21]

Bill Clinton made clear in his 1992 presidential campaign that he would pursue a foreign policy similar to, if not more expansive than, that of the Bush administration. In 1993 his secretary of state-designate, Warren Christopher, addressed a group of neoconservative Democrats, including Penn Kimball, Joshua Muravchik, Peter Rosenblatt, Albert Shanker, and Max Kampelman, to assure them that he would fully back the president's commitments to make promotion of democracy a central tenet of U.S. foreign policy.[22] Christopher's successor, Madeleine Albright, was even more comfortable with this stance. Democratist ideology was by now clearly dominant in top policymaking circles in Washington and elsewhere. It both generated and sanctioned an assertive, expansive use of American power.

When running for president, George W. Bush appeared to have substantial reservations about this broad, interventionist use of American might. He questioned the desire to impose solutions in all regional and local trouble spots around the world and to undertake "nation-building," seeming to recognize that such efforts betrayed arrogance and an undue will to power that other countries might resent. In his campaign for the presidency, George W. Bush said repeatedly that the United States needed a more "humble" foreign policy. His adoption of a wholly different, far more assertive tone after the 9/11 attacks was surely induced in large part by warlike conditions. Although the change was probably motivated more by pragmatic than by ideological considerations, President Bush's rhetoric began to take on a neo-Jacobin coloring, as when he spoke of the "axis of evil," a phrase coined by neoconservative speechwriter David Frum.

In subsequent speeches, the president has come to resemble Woodrow Wilson in assigning to the United States, the exceptional country, an exceptional mission in the world. He has asserted that an attack upon the United States is an attack upon freedom: "A lot of young people say, 'Well, Why America? Why would anybody want to come after us?' And the answer is because we love freedom, that's why. And they hate freedom." Identifying America with the universal cause of freedom, Bush even adopted the imagery of Wilson. The American flag stands, he said, "not only for our power, but for freedom."[23] Although the president used the term "freedom" rather than "democracy," which is the one favored by the new Jacobins, he seemed to agree with the notion that any enemy or critic of the United States is the opponent of universal principle: "They have attacked America, because we are freedom's home and defender."[24]

Proponents of American empire had moved with great speed to head off any reluctance on the part of a devastated and disoriented American public to deal quickly and comprehensively with terrorism and its supporters around the globe. Already on the morning after the attacks, when it was still not clear who was responsible, the *Washington Post* carried an article by Robert Kagan calling for sweeping countermeasures. The U.S. Congress should, Kagan insisted, declare war immediately on the terrorists and any nation that might have assisted them. The situation required that America act with "moral clarity and courage as our grandfathers did [responding to the attack on Pearl Harbor]. Not by asking what we have done to bring on the wrath of inhuman murderers. Not by figuring out ways to reason with, or try to appease those who have spilled our blood."[25] On the same day William Bennett, Jack Kemp, and Jeane Kirkpatrick issued a statement calling for war against the "entire" Islamic terrorist network.[26]

If the president thought that American actions might have anything to do with so much hostility to the United States in the world, he did not, and in the circumstances perhaps could not, say so publicly. What he did say and said repeatedly is that the United States must be diligent, active, and forceful—preemptive even—in dealing with present or potential threats of terrorism. Paradoxically, given his earlier calls for American humility, he presided over a massive push for greater American involvement in the world and for a much expanded and also much more intrusive role for government in the daily lives of U.S. citizens. In fairness to a politician who is not also an intellectual and a historian, war has its own logic, and he may have been insufficiently aware of the full implications of his policy statements. But President Bush's assertive approach and universalistic rhetoric was seized on by American democratists who had been preparing the ground for war and for a wider pursuit of empire. In a *Washington Post* column titled "Peace Through Democracy," Charles Krauthammer praised the president for applying "the fundamental principle of American foreign policy—the promotion of democracy."[27] The political activist and writer Midge Decter pointed out that after 9/11 America could do something to clean up the world. She urged her countrymen "to hang onto what is most important to remember: that our country, the strongest on earth, has been pressed by circumstance—I would say, has been granted the opportunity—to rid the world of some goodly measure of its cruelty and pestilence."[28]

In mid-September, 2002, President Bush sent to the U.S. Congress the president's annual statement on strategy, "The National Security Strategy of the United States of America," which gave clear evidence that he was abandoning his earlier calls for a more "humble" U.S. foreign policy. Though the report was framed as a strategy for combating terrorism, the stated objectives supererogated any need to respond to acute external or internal threats. The report defined what amounted to a new and highly ambitious role for America in the world. Released the day after the president asked the Congress to authorize the use of preemptive military force against Iraq, it provided justifications for American intervention against potential security threats, while formulating a much broader international agenda. The report in effect set forth a doctrine of American armed hegemony. The president justified this ascendancy as serving both America's security needs and its efforts to promote freedom, democracy, and free trade. The *Washington Post* said that the report gave the United States "a nearly messianic role." It meant not only acceptance but also an extension of the old Wolfowitz draft plan. Indeed, Wolfowitz was now deputy secretary of defense and a highly vocal and assertive proponent of American activism around the world. According to the report, America's strength and influence in the world is "unprecedented" and "unequalled." The United States, "sustained by faith in the principles of liberty and the value of a free society," also has "unparalleled responsibilities, obligations and opportunities" beyond its borders. The report called for possessing such overwhelming military power as to discourage any other power from challenging American hegemony or developing weapons of mass destruction. It overturned the old doctrines of deterrence and containment. Committing the United States to a much-expanded understanding of security, it argued that the United States must reserve the right to act preemptively and unilaterally against potentially threatening states or organizations. "We will be prepared to act apart when our interests and unique responsibilities require." But the president approved an even wider goal. He committed the United States to making the world "not just safer but better." In explaining the report, a senior administration official said that besides leading the world in the war against terrorists and "aggressive regimes seeking weapons of mass destruction," the United States should preserve the peace, "extend the benefits of liberty and prosperity through the spread of American values," and promote "good governance." In familiar-sounding words, the report described America's strategy as a "distinctly American internationalism that reflects the union of our values and our national interests."[29]

September 11 outraged the president. It shifted the focus of his attention to world affairs. It gave him a new sense of the military and other power at his disposal. It was also a powerful stimulus for such nationalistic inclinations as he had. Yet it is not likely that George W. Bush would have changed his approach to foreign policy so drastically relative to his election campaign, had he not been affected by the ideology of empire, as transmitted to him by some of his advisors and speechwriters. The attack on America could have elicited a strong but surgical and limited response; it became instead the occasion and justification for launching a drive for something grndiose.

The humility in foreign policy that President Bush had earlier advocated was no longer visible. In an interview about a year after the attack, he said, "The United States is in a unique position right now. We are the leader." Neither, apparently, was humility a marked feature of his personal demeanor. Asked whether, in discussions with his advisors, he ever explained to them his position or intentions, he answered, "Of course not. I'm the commander—see I don't need to explain—I do not need to explain why I say things. That's the interesting thing about being the president. Maybe somebody needs to explain to me why they say something, but I don't feel like I owe anybody an explanation."[30]

The time had long been ripe for the neo-Jacobin vision of virtuous empire to be fully and systematically implemented in U.S. foreign policy. The election of George W. Bush as president had seemed at first a setback for the new Jacobins, for he had advocated a more restrictive use of American power, but if Bush had done so out of genuine conviction rather than expediency, 9/11 brought a profound change of heart. The already available ideology of empire helped remove any inhibitions the president might have had about an activist foreign policy and helped shape his reaction to the attack. It can be debated to what extent his advisors and speechwriters, who were to varying degrees attracted to the ideology, along with numerous media commentators of the same orientation, were able to channel the president's anger, but the new Jacobins took full advantage of 9/11 to advance their long-standing quest for empire. Knowingly or unknowingly, the president of the United States moved to embrace the idea of armed world hegemony. He became their leading spokesman, and he received their very strong support.

The foreign policy of George W. Bush's immediate two predecessors, Bush, Sr. and Bill Clinton, had had a strong Wilsonian tilt, but neither president had followed any sustained, consistent strategy. By contrast, the Bush doctrine, as set forth in the "National Security Strategy," committed the United States to a bold, comprehensive, and elaborate foreign policy. The publicly and formally stated U.S. goal, in sum, was to establish global supremacy. The United States would set itself up as the arbiter of good and evil in the world and, if necessary, enforce its judgments unilaterally.

The spread of freedom was closely associated in the president's mind with using American military might. In June of 2001 he informed the Congress that the "Department of Defense has become the most powerful force for freedom the world has ever seen."[31] His words recall the statement by Rousseau that those who are not on the side of political right must be "forced to be free." In January of 2003, in a speech to troops preparing for war against Iraq, the president said, "You'll be fighting not to conquer anybody, but to liberate people."[32] In the ensuing State of the Union Address, in a passage addressed to American soldiers preparing for invasion of Iraq, he again extolled the selflessness of the United States: "America is a strong nation and honorable in the use of our strength. We exercise power without conquest, and we sacrifice for the liberty of strangers." Dropping even the appearance of humility, the president went on to say with a mixture of Wilsonian self-congratulation and messianic self-importance: "Americans are a free people, who know that freedom is the right of every person and the future of every nation. The liberty we praise is not America's gift to the world; it is God's gift to humanity."[33]

Reservations expressed in Europe and elsewhere about American unilateralism and global aspirations were scorned and dismissed by proponents of empire as a failure to recognize the need to combat evil in the world. Kenneth Adelman, a former deputy U.S. Ambassador to the United Nations and a highly placed advisor on defense to the U.S. government, couched his advocacy of imperial designs in terms of fighting terrorism: "I don't think Europeans should cooperate with the United States as a favor to the United States. They should be very grateful to the United States and cooperate because we have a common enemy—terrorism. In my mind, it's a decisive moment in the conflict between civilization and barbarism."[34] Again, America was on the side of good, and those not willing simply to follow America's lead were aiding and abetting evil.

The belief in American moral superiority knows no party lines. In an article critical of the George W. Bush administration's way of preparing for war against Iraq, Richard C. Holbrooke, United States ambassador to the United Nations under President Clinton, expressed a view ubiquitous in the American foreign policy establishment: "Over the past 60 years, the United States has consistently combined its military superiority with moral and political leadership."[35] Consistently? The notion that, unlike other nations, America is above moral suspicion, provides the best possible justification for exercising American power.

It seems to proponents of the ideology of American empire that, surely, America the virtuous is entitled to dominate the world. Some of them have worked long and hard to make this point of view dominant in American foreign policy. President Bush was merely echoing what others had been saying when he stated: "There is a value system that cannot be compromised, and that is the values we praise. And if the values are good enough for our people, they ought to be good enough for others."[36]

Many members of the so-called Christian right share the view that America has a special mission, but give this notion a triumphalist religious cast beyond the moralism typical of neo-Jacobin ideology. They believe that the United States, as led by a man of God, has a virtually messianic role to play, especially in the Middle East, where God's chosen people, Israel, must be supported by the United States against their enemies. Breaking sharply with the mainstream of traditional Christianity, which has made a distinction between the things of God and the things of Caesar, this form of religion identifies a particular political power, America, with God's will. George W. Bush's rhetoric often suggested that he was strongly drawn to such thinking. He even indicated that he saw himself and the armed forces of the United States as bringing to the peoples of the world the kind of deliverance from bondage for which the Jewish people longed in the Old Testament. Announcing the end of major combat operations in Iraq, the president thanked "this generation of the military" for having "taken up the highest calling of history," which is to "bring liberty to others." "Wherever you go," he told the soldiers, "you carry a message of hope." He then explained this message in a sentence in which he quoted Scripture: "In the words of the prophet Isaiah: To the captives, 'Come out,' and to those in darkness, 'Be free.'"[37] A work of liberation that had traditionally been associated with God and interpreted as chiefly spiritual was thus assigned to the commander in chief and the soldiers of the U.S Armed Forces. A religious longing had been conflated with a political cause.

"Evangelical" Christianity of the kind that seemed to appeal to President Bush may rest on simplistic theological, biblical, and historical assumptions and have virtually no influence over America's dominant national culture—the big media, the leading universities, the art world, and the movie, music, and publishing industries—but it provides considerable political support for neo-Jacobinism, which does have such influence. In its practical effects on United States foreign policy, this religious triumphalism puts a religious gloss on neo-Jacobinism. It does not Christianize Unites States foreign policy, but makes it less humble and more belligerent.

Not all who reflect neo-Jacobin thinking in foreign affairs and contribute to its political advance are fully conscious of the role they play or of its long-term significance. Some powerful persons who are not intellectuals and have limited knowledge of philosophy and history are rather easily manipulated and pressured. Of those who give voice to neo-Jacobin ideas far from all are acting and speaking out of intense ideological commitment, though many clearly are. Also, some individuals who spend most of their time thinking about foreign policy and international affairs may be only vaguely aware of how their ideas relate to general issues of political thought and of how the neo-Jacobin impulse manifests itself in other areas. One of the aims of this book is to show the connection between ideas that may, superficially viewed, look unrelated. The main objective here continues to be to demonstrate the general intellectual-political dynamic of neo-Jacobin thinking and the nature and extent of its influence in transforming America and the world. To decide precisely who is and who is not a fully-fledged representative of this ideology is in the context of this book less important.

Both in domestic and international affairs the new Jacobins are strongly prejudiced against the traditions of old, historically evolved nations and groups. These are seen as retarding the emergence of a new order based on what the new Jacobins consider universal principles. In their view, the distinctive traits of different societies and cultures should yield to the homogeneity of virtuous democracy. The new Jacobins are trying to clear away obstacles to the triumph of their ideology and of their own will to power. In light of their anti-traditionalism, it may seem paradoxical that, in political practice, they often target regimes that are not particularly traditional, though they rule societies of a more traditional cast. It must be understood that the neo-Jacobins are hostile to *all* significant opposition to their own vision, not least when it comes from radical regimes in other societies that constitute a significant obstacle to the realization of their own plans. The new Jacobins postpone dealing with more traditional but unobtrusive regimes in order to take on more direct and powerful competition.

Neo-Jacobins cite the perniciousness of particular regimes as a justification for removing them, but the suffering visited upon a people by the despised regime may be limited compared to the death and destruction inflicted by the avenging angel of neo-Jacobinism, despite the fact that she is armed with precision bombs and other "smart" weapons. War has sometimes incalculable costs. The new Jacobins consider thousands of dead and wounded and other devastation an acceptable price for bringing down an abhorrent regime and installing "democracy." Whether the people in question agree seems to them an irrelevant question. Good must triumph over evil, as they understand them, and evil is always on the other side. It is necessary to ask: What limit, if any, will the new Jacobins be willing to place on the human cost for their reign of virtue?

An observer who finds a regime targeted by the neo-Jacobins abhorrent might comment that, surely, neo-Jacobin intervention is less objectionable than the continuation of the regime. Comparing the stated neo-Jacobin goals for the particular society with its present sad state of affairs, such an observer easily forgets that "goals" are indistinguishable from their probable consequences and are never meaningfully assessed purely in the abstract. The violence and destruction that may be necessary in the attempt to realize the goals are an integral part of what they are. If goals are ill-conceived or poorly adapted to the particular historical situation, the result of acting on them can be disastrous. A reason for the utter inhumanity of communism is that it tried to realize aims that were simply unattainable. The practice of communism revealed much about the true nature of its stated goals. Neo-Jacobinism is similarly convinced that it has the right prescription for all societies. Its aims, too, are subject to the same reality check. Here it is appropriate to consider that while a leader or regime in the so-called "rogue" category typically has very limited resources and usually restrict his ruthlessness to his own societies or the immediate region, America's mistakes in promoting high-sounding ideals can have the most profound and long-lasting consequences.

There are in the world, besides the millions of people who have become intensely hostile to the United States, also some who think that American interventionism may be a good counter to such movements as quasi-Islamic radicalism. People who think that way are typically pro-American since the Second World War or the Cold War. They assume that the America that is now pursuing an activist foreign policy is much the same as the one that they once idealized. The neo-Jacobins are able to make use of the credibility and good will built up by Americans of a different kind. Also, an older America, with roots in traditional Western and Anglo-American civilization and with a general ethos sharply at odds with that of the new Jacobinism, still survives, though in greatly weakened form. It has not lost all influence over American policy. The enactment of neo-Jacobin foreign policy initiatives falls in large part to people who are not on the neo-Jacobin bandwagon, specifically, many in the Armed Forces of the United States, the State Department and the Central Intelligence Agency. The officer corps is perhaps the American social group with the closest religious, moral and cultural ties to a more traditional America. As long as people of that kind can moderate and humanize neo-Jacobin designs, American policy will be more cautious and circumspect than if it were wholly dominated, in the implementation as well as the formulation, by the new Jacobins. Though loyal to their civilian superiors, most American officers are still skeptical of the idea of American empire and interventionism.

To understand the theoretical and practical import of neo-Jacobinism it is important to try to discern what this movement is in itself, when it operates according to its own inner momentum. What would America be like, internationally and domestically, if neo-Jacobinism became more firmly entrenched? Its uncompromising virtue would then no longer be impeded by the traditional influences that it resents. There are strong philosophical and historical reasons to expect such an America to become more and more ruthless in pursuit of its objectives, whatever their rhetorical appearance.

Even if the opinions examined in this chapter are assessed in the most generous and charitable spirit, their element of political-ideological imperialism is hard to miss. A philosophically and historically inclined observer is reminded of the terrible and large-scale suffering that has been inflicted on mankind by power-seeking sanctioned or inspired by one or another kind of Jacobin moral and intellectual conceit. Communism, one of the most radical and pernicious manifestations of the Jacobin spirit, has disintegrated, at least as a major political force, but another panacea for the world is taking its place. The neo-Jacobin vision for how to redeem humanity may be less obviously utopian and inhumane than that of communism. It may strike some as admirably idealistic, as did communism. But, as will be shown more fully in the next chapter, the two visions are not quite so different as they may appear. The spirit of the two movements is similar, and utopian thinking is utopian thinking, fairly innocuous perhaps if restricted to isolated dreamers and theoreticians but dangerous to the extent that it inspires action in the real world. The concern voiced here is that neo-Jacobinism has come to permeate American public debate and is finally within reach of controlling the military might of the United States.

Prudence, realism, compromise, and self-restraint are indispensable qualities in politics. They have been reflected in traditional American institutions, in great decisions made by American statesmen, and sometimes in American public opinion. They have constituted the first line of defense against all manner of foreign and domestic threats, including surges of passion and eruptions of extremism. Given the atrocities of 9/11 and the need for a firm American response, the prominence of crusaders in the Bush administration was perhaps not surprising, but it was also a sign that needed old American virtues are weakening or disappearing. The continued ascendancy of neo-Jacobinism would have disastrous consequences. By acting under its influence America's leaders may be setting in motion fateful developments that they and their successors will not be able to control.

Notes

1. James David Barber, *Washington Post*, January 25, 1990.
2. Charles Krauthammer, *Washington Post*, June 21, 1991.
3. Ben Wattenberg, *Washington Times*, March 21, 1990.
4. Francis Fukuyama, "End of History."
5. Quoted in Bruce Mazlish, *The Revolutionary Ascetic* (New York: Basic Books, 1976), 86.
6. Bloom, *Closing*, 153.
7. For a philosophical discussion of the preconditions of peace and respectful relations among societies and cultures, see *Common Human Ground*
8. William Kristol and David Brooks, *Wall Street Journal*, September 15, 1997.
9. Robert Kagan, *Washington Post*, May 26, 2002.
10. Kristol and Brooks, *Wall Street Journal*, September 15, 1997.
11. Ben Wattenberg, *Washington Times,* December 1, 1988, August 8 and 1, 1990 (emphasis added).
12. Ben Wattenberg, *Washington Times*, March 21, 1990.
13. Charles Krauthammer, *Washington Post*, March 22, 1991.
14. Michael Novak, *The Washington Times,* December 23, 1988.
15. Irving Babbitt, *Democracy and Leadership* (Indianapolis, IN: Liberty Fund, 1979; first published in 1924), 337, 295. It is a national misfortune that Americans have paid less attention to one of their truly great thinkers than to a number of lesser European lights who impress by their denser, more technical, less essayistic philosophical style.

16. Woodrow Wilson, Thanksgiving Proclamation, November 7, 1917, *The Papers of Woodrow Wilson,* Arthur S. Link et al. (Princeton, NJ: Princeton University Press, 1966-93), 44, 525; and Address at Independence Hall, Philadelphia, *Papers,* 30, 254. For an in-depth study of Woodrow Wilson and his notion of America as servant of mankind, see Richard M. Gamble, "Savior Nation: Woodrow Wilson and the Gospel of Service," *Humanitas,* Vol. XIV, No. 1 (2001).

17. Babbitt, *Democracy,* 314.

18. Secretary of State James A. Baker, speech to the Aspen Institute in Berlin, Germany, June 18, 1991.

19. *New York Times,* March 8, 1992.

20. *Washington Post,* March 13, 1992.

21. *Wall Street Journal,* lead editorial, March 16, 1992.

22. *Washington Post,* January 9, 1993. The designation "neoconservative" for the mentioned individuals is taken from this article.

23. *Washington Post,* June 23, 2002.

24. Remarks, National Cathedral, September 14, 2001.

25. *Washington Post,* September 12, 2001.

26. Statement of three of the co-directors of Empower America, September 12, 2001.

27. Charles Krauthammer, *Washington Post,* June 28, 2002.

28. Midge Decter, *Imprimis,* vol. 31, no. 9 (September 2002), 5.

29. The President's annual strategy statement to the U.S. Congress, "National Security Strategy of the United States of America," September 17, 2002, and *Washington Post,* September 21, 2002.

30. Remarks by President George W. Bush in interview with Bob Woodward, *Washington Post,* November 19, 2002.

31. Statement to the U.S. Congress, June 18, 2001.

32. George W. Bush, presidential address, Fort Hood, January 3, 2003.

33. George W. Bush, State of the Union Address, Jan 28, 2003.

34. *Washington Post,* "Outlook" section, September 29, 2002

35. Richard C. Hoolbrooke, "It Did Not Have to Be This Way," *Washington Post,* February 23, 2003.

36. Remarks by President George W. Bush, in taped interview with Bob Woodward, *Washington Post,* November 19, 2002; excerpted from Woodward, *Bush at War.*

37. George W. Bush, speech to the nation, "America Is Grateful for a Job Well Done," *Washington Post,* May 2, 2003.

14

Jacobin Capitalism

"The bourgeoisie, by the rapid improvement of all instruments of production, by the immensely facilitated means of communication, draws all, even the most barbarian, nations into civilization . . . It compels all nations, on pain of extinction, to adopt the bourgeois mode of production; it compels them to introduce what it calls civilization into their midst, i.e., to become bourgeois themselves. In one word, it creates a world after its own image."—Karl Marx[1]

An important component of what the new Jacobins advocate is what they call "capitalism" or "free markets." These are considered closely akin to "democracy." Often the terms "democracy" and "capitalism" are used almost interchangeably. They are taken as names for different but closely linked dimensions of one and the same desirable society. Michael Novak popularized the term "democratic capitalism." Like democracy, capitalism should be introduced into all countries for the good of the inhabitants. Unfortunately, the term "capitalism" is as mired in philosophical confusion as is "democracy." The way in which advocacy of capitalism can be an outlet for the Jacobin spirit may be explained by demonstrating that there are major moral and theoretical connections between certain current notions of capitalism and the ideas of the French Revolution.

In their effort to bestow their allegedly noble insights on people far and wide, the French Jacobins combined adherence to abstract ideals with moralistic righteousness. Warnings from others, including Edmund Burke, that in the reform of society concrete circumstances and historical experience had to be taken into account and respected, seemed to the French revolutionaries morally perverse and reactionary. No guide was necessary other than their own universal principles. To liberate mankind from oppression and enact freedom, equality, and brotherhood, a clean break with the past was necessary. Jean-Jacques Rousseau had shown the need to abandon not only old beliefs but also all of the social and political structures from which they were indistinguishable. Western civilization could not be dismantled without destroying the concrete institutional and other arrangements through which it expressed itself.

The notion that all historically existing societies are full of exploitation and other evils and that a society of justice and well-being can be created only through sweeping and radical change has appeared in many versions since the time of the French Jacobins. The words "left" and "right" used to indicate the extent to which particular individuals and movements were drawn to that notion—the "left" finding it morally appealing and intellectually persuasive, the "right" finding it both morally repugnant and philosophically untenable. Today, sentiments of this kind are common across the political-intellectual spectrum. Indeed, some people called conservatives are in the forefront of those offering solutions for the world's ills. Conservatives used to be highly skeptical of sweeping proposals for changing society or the world; they reacted viscerally against panaceas and cant. They seemed to enthusiastic reformers to be spoilsports and killjoys. They drew attention to inconvenient facts and stated uncomfortable truths. The conservatives of the new kind are not so unpleasant and ornery. In fact, optimism and a belief in uninterrupted progress are their hallmarks. They propose political and economic programs that appear quite different from those advocated by the conventional left, and they usually speak a different language, but they share with the old left a belief in the salvific power and universal applicability of their programs. They envision ultimate goals for society that bear a much stronger resemblance to those of the old Jacobins than might first appear.

The Jacobin spirit found an uncompromising particular form in Marxism. Since Karl Marx looked forward to the destruction of capitalism and the triumph of socialism and communism, it might seem that a defender of capitalism could have little in common with the new Jacobinism. It is time again to insist on the need for distinctions and to point out that, like "free market," the term "capitalism" can have sharply different meanings. It should not be forgotten that a desire among the French middle classes to be rid of various old restrictions on commerce was among the major impulses behind the

French Revolution. In today's Western society, the wish for economic freedom has been taken to an extreme by various radical "libertarians." It should be carefully noted that there is a sense in which a free market would become a reality only if the movement of goods and services were wholly unrestricted, unfettered not only by "external," legal, or institutional checks but by "inner" restraints, such as the inhibitions and tastes of civilized persons. A Rousseauistic, Jacobin desire to destroy traditional moral and cultural restraints and corresponding sociopolitical structures can thus be said to aid in the creation of a truly free market. It is not far-fetched but entirely consistent to be a moral, intellectual, and cultural radical and a strong proponent of the free market—by a certain definition of "free market."

Of those in the West today who are passionate advocates of capitalism and want it introduced all over the world, many are former Marxists. The shift from being a Marxist to becoming a missionary for capitalism may be less drastic than is commonly assumed. Depending on the definition of capitalism, there can be considerable continuity between the first and the second position.

It should be recognized, first of all, that, although Karl Marx predicted the replacement of capitalism by socialism and then by the stateless society of communism, he was a great admirer of capitalism. Like today's proponents of capitalism he credited it with unleashing enormous productive power. In the words of *The Communist Manifesto* (1848), "The bourgeoisie, during its rule of scarce one hundred years, has created more massive and more colossal productive forces than have all preceding generations together." Far from opposing the spread of capitalism, Marx believed, again like today's enthusiastic champions of capitalism, that it must expand across the globe. It will lift mankind to a new level of development. For Marx, capitalism makes all peoples the beneficiaries of the historical progress that will finally end the suffering of mankind: "The bourgeoisie, by the rapid improvement of all instruments of production, by the immensely facilitated means of communication, draws all, even the most barbarian, nations into civilization." By "civilization" Marx here meant the productive potential of modern industrialized society.[2]

The parallels between Marx and some of today's missionaries for capitalism are thus evident. An obvious difference is that Marx sees capitalism as causing great travail. He regards the revolution of the proletariat and the overthrow of capitalism as necessary for mankind's final liberation. An important question to ask about particular proponents of capitalism today is whether they reject the doctrines of Karl Marx because of fundamental disagreements with his view of man, society, and history, or because they *share* much of his moral pathos but believe that the desirable society can be more efficiently achieved by avoiding revolution and socialism as he thought of them. A person may advocate capitalism not so much because he utterly rejects Marx's vision of a new society as because he regards the revolution of the proletariat and the socialist organization of production as blind alleys, quite unnecessary for realizing an essentially egalitarian society freed of the prejudices, injustices, and constraints of traditional civilization. A person may endorse capitalism because letting the market do its work is the best way of uprooting backward beliefs and related sociopolitical structures. Note carefully that, for Marx himself, one of the most important features of capitalism, as he understands it, is that it will completely destroy traditional civilization, not just in the Western world but wherever it takes hold.

A Jacobin in spirit could thus become an enthusiastic advocate of capitalism—provided capitalism is expected to function in a particular way. The destruction of old-fashioned civilized life that capitalism of this type brings with it is similar to that effected by plebiscitary democracy. In the end, the old decentralized and group-oriented society and the ethical, intellectual, and cultural beliefs that fostered it are left in ruins. It was the possibility of a capitalism of this kind that created unease about the free market not just in the old Roman Catholic Church and among Christians generally but among all who treasured the old heritage of humane civilization. Joseph Schumpeter, himself an admirer of the productive efficiency of capitalism, feared its capacity for destroying desirable features of traditional society. Capitalism pushes all but economic considerations aside. "Bourgeois society," he wrote, "has been cast in a purely economic mold: its foundations, beams and beacons are all made of economic material." In this society prizes and penalties are measured in pecuniary terms: "The promises of wealth and the threats of destitution that it holds out, it redeems with ruthless promptitude."[3] These observers of capitalism may be criticized for having had a one-sided and reductionist view of capitalism, but they did call attention to real potentialities of the economic system. Misgivings about such manifestations of capitalism continue to be strongly felt not just by socialists but also by friends of the free market who also believe that it ought to be integrated into and bounded by the higher purposes of civilization.

The Jacobin spirit can align itself with and try to boost those potentialities of capitalism that are most destructive of the ways of traditional society. It can do so in part by seizing upon and giving wider circulation to vague, nice-sounding, but sophistical notions like "equality of economic opportunity," "equality at the starting line," or "a level playing field." Because most people, especially in the United States, spontaneously oppose obstacles to opportunity that are unreasonable, irrelevant to tasks to be performed, or otherwise artificial, it is easily overlooked that, if taken quite seriously and literally, equality of economic opportunity requires a radical transformation of society. It requires the removal of all those considerations that, in traditional civilization, limit and structure economic activity so as to make it compatible with or supportive of humane values that lie beyond supply and demand. Equality of opportunity, taken literally, means treating all persons—moral and immoral, noble and ignoble, crude and refined—equally as long as they perform adequately by some narrowly economic, utilitarian standard. Other types of criteria should be set aside.

But civilization depends on *not* letting purely economic considerations dominate society. The logic of equality of opportunity is to drive out extra-economic standards, to remove premiums and penalties that nudge or force individuals to be of one kind rather than another. A couple of random examples may suggest the practical consequences of carrying equality of economic opportunity to its ultimate conclusion. The tax codes of all countries favor and disfavor some social arrangements. This is to slant economic opportunity, to make it unequal. Real equality would require, for instance, that families and homeowners be given no tax benefits not available to all others, including young singles and persons uninterested in the rootedness of home ownership. In business, equality of opportunity would mean that decisions to hire and promote should not favor the responsible, courteous, well-groomed individual over the slick, ill-mannered, sloppy person except insofar as the difference might affect productivity. In professional sports, the personally odious player should have the same chance to play and make money as the one who sets an example for others, as long as their professional skills are comparable. To bring about real equality it would be necessary to go down a very long list of changes until society has been drained of every civilized preference—which means that civilization will have ceased to exist.

The phrase "a level playing field" as a description of capitalism (or, for that matter, democracy) may seem rather innocuous. As used by some, it might mean simply that no one should have an unfair advantage over another. People of privilege should not be able to deny others the advancement and the rewards to which they are entitled by natural ability and hard work. Clearly, a soundly traditional society needs counterweights to social inbreeding, stagnation, and snobbery. All societies need the revivification of institutions and behavior that comes from challenges to old ways. Balancing the need for continuity and the need for change is a great task of civilization. But what is unfair advantage? Civilization attempts to enact its preferences precisely by giving advantages and encouragement to some, namely to those who come closest to embodying the values central to civilization, and placing obstacles in the way of others, namely those who deliberately and egregiously threaten those values. Except in a special, limited sense, civilization does not aim to treat people equally. Doing so would be unjust, for no two individuals are the same or have the same merit. Only a government based on great moral and intellectual conceit would consider it possible to ensure by central direction that all persons receive their just deserts, whatever the standard of fairness employed. Such a government would have to adopt totalitarian methods. Nevertheless, it is a general aim of civilization to structure life so that, to the greatest extent possible, those who enjoy or acquire advantages and influence are also, by the highest standards, deserving of them—which is far less a matter of political control than of decentralized, diversified, slow, protracted, piecemeal historical selection and adjustment. What is appealing to the Jacobin about the term "level playing field" is that it suggests the absence of traditional sociopolitical patterns that encourage some types of behavior and discourage others. As used by the modern Jacobin, the phrase indicates a society swept free of the discriminations between high and low through which civilization defines, manifests and preserves itself.

Ensuring real equality of economic opportunity as understood by the Jacobin would obviously require much interference with the economy as it exists in actual societies. Taken literally and seriously, the mentioned notions of equality of opportunity must, in practice, result in great expansion of the administrative state and in the eventual blending of capitalism and socialism. If capitalism means "equality at the starting line" and the latter is assumed actually to mean what it says, capitalism requires, among other things, the abolition of inheritance, which gives the children of the well-to-do an advantage over others. A certain kind of advocacy of capitalism turns out to have much in common with the Jacobin passion for an egalitarian, homogeneous society.

But it is possible to understand capitalism, or the free market, very differently. There is a need to distinguish between different forms of the free economy along lines similar to the distinction between constitutional and plebiscitary democracy. A free market of goods and services may exist in a decentralized, group-oriented society in which the outlook and behavior of individuals and firms are leavened by moral and other disciplines and in which both supply and demand are structured by corresponding civilized desires. In this economy, relations between competitors may be softened by mutual respect and consideration. A free market of this type would share in the ethos that is also characteristic of constitutional government. It would be an integral part of the civilized society with its institutionally expressed likes and dislikes.

The vital importance of the social setting of the market was stressed by the economist Wilhelm Röpke (1899-1966). "The market economy is one thing in a society where atomization, mass, proletarianization, and concentration rule," in which moral rootlessness robs competition of traditional ethical restraints, and in which producers cater indiscriminately to consumer demand. The market can be quite another thing, Röpke insisted, in the kind of decentralized, group-centered society that was described earlier in this book as fostering the character on which constitutionalism depends. "In such a society," Röpke wrote, "wealth would be widely dispersed; people's lives would have solid foundations; genuine communities, from the family upward, would form a background of moral support for the individual; there would be counterweights to competition and the mechanical operation of prices; people would have roots and would not be adrift in life without anchor."[4]

It must be understood that the distinction here developed between two forms of capitalism, or the market, is not between slightly different versions of one and the same economic system. It is a distinction between opposed potentialities that are no more compatible than are constitutional and plebiscitary democracy.

Critics of capitalism typically identify it with its worst possibilities: ruthless competition, exploitation, greed, crude commercialism, social atomism, and so on. These are said to be of the very essence of a free economy. That such phenomena are prominent in a particular economy is actually but a sign that capitalism is operating within a society in which people lack ethical, aesthetical, and other inhibitions and strong communal ties, a society in which institutional structures do not embody civilized purposes and in which neither supply nor demand recognizes any higher standards. Critics of democracy similarly identify democracy with its worst potentialities: unchecked majoritarianism, political irresponsibility, demagoguery, pandering to the lowest common denominator, and so on. Here, too, the phenomenon in question, democracy, is alleged to have its essence in how it performs in a society where civilized restraints are weak. Both points of view are unhistorical and reductionist. In reality, capitalism and democracy have no single definition or "essence." They exist only in particular historical manifestations. These can be sharply different depending on the ethical and cultural health of the particular society in which they operate. They can be compatible with the ends of a good society, in which case their institutions and practices are integral to the structures and practices of civilization. But they can also be destructive of higher values, in which case they manifest the structures and practices of a deteriorating society.

Röpke has described the social setting of a desirable free economy in a way that shows its connection with what was earlier explained as the moral and cultural context of constitutional popular government:

> Self-discipline, a sense of justice, honesty, fairness, chivalry, moderation, public spirit, respect for human dignity, firm ethical norms—all of these are things which people must possess before they go to market and compete with each other. These are the indispensable supports which preserve both market and competition from degeneration. Family,

church, genuine communities, and tradition are their sources. It is also necessary that people should grow up in conditions which favor such moral convictions, conditions of a natural order, conditions promoting co-operation, respecting tradition, and giving moral support to the individual. . . . It is the foundation upon which the ethics of the market economy must rest. It is an order which fosters individual independence and responsibility as much as the public spirit which connects the individual with the community and limits his greed.[5]

This book has argued that constitutional democracy has demanding ethical and cultural prerequisites and that it is not easily created and maintained. In a morally and culturally deteriorating society there is a great likelihood that democracy will be transformed into a plebiscitary regime, though one not answering to the Rousseauistic ideal of active, virtuous citizenship but relying on long-distance government. Among those with discriminating standards, popular passivity and abdication of power, together with the moral and cultural changes that lie behind them, will begin to give popular government a bad name. A similar argument can be made with regard to the free market. If the people who produce and consume cease to exhibit the discipline and responsibility characteristic of a civilized society, the free market, too, will, even if it continues to produce goods and services, begin to give itself a bad reputation among people who in trying to enrich civilization look beyond quantitative standards.

When observers inside and outside of the Roman Catholic Church expressed reservations about the free market, these were, in the final analysis, concerns about more general developments in Western civilization. Warnings about the possible dangers of the free economy could just as well have been directed against parallel dangers posed by other social freedoms and by popular government. The dangers did not inhere in the free market "as such," for no such market exists. They inhered in the free market in a particular part of the world and in a particular historical period, whose moral and other standards were becoming shaky.

As aligned with and shaped by a spirit of radicalism, capitalism can do much to obliterate traditional moral and cultural standards and uproot traditional communities. For some of today's proponents of capitalism one of its appeals is precisely that it can efficiently accomplish a task of destruction. Behind praise for capitalism one may find, among other things, resentment against traditional elites and a desire to sweep from positions of influence people who are seen as upholding old-fashioned, more aristocratic standards. Simultaneous advocacy of capitalism and majoritarian democracy broadens and intensifies the attack upon the old society. The spirit of Rousseau and Marx, if not all of their specific ideas, has in this way been updated and adjusted to new historical circumstances, and it has here found plentiful new opportunities.

Notes

1. Karl Marx and Friedrich Engels, *The Communist Manifesto* (Harmondsworth: Penguin Books, 1974), 84.
2. Ibid., 85.
3. Joseph Schumpeter, *Capitalism, Socialism and Democracy* (New York: Harper, 1950; first published in 1942), 73. The book exudes a melancholy pessimism about the future of capitalism. For examples of official Roman Catholic concern about the dangers of capitalism before the Church became heavily influenced by a socialist view of capitalism, see the Papal encyclicals *Rerum Novarum* (1891) and *Quadragesimo Anno* (1931).
4. Wilhelm Röpke, A *Humane Economy* (Wilmington, DE: Intercollegiate Studies Institute, 1998), 35. See also, Röpke, *The Moral Foundations of Civil Society* (New Brunswick, NJ: Transaction Publishers, 1996).
5. Röpke, *Economy,* 125. For a brief but philosophically lucid and incisive discussion of the relationship between ethics and economics, see Joseph Baldacchino, *Economics and the Moral Order* (Washington, DC: National Humanities Institute, 1985).

15

Equality

"The idea of Equality, as expressed in the Declaration of Independence, is the key to the morality of 'the laws of nature and of nature's God.' It is this natural law which the Constitution . . . is designed to implement."—Harry Jaffa[1]

The examination and analysis of the new Jacobinism has shown it to be a reasonably coherent ideology built around several closely connected ideas, including "equality," "virtue," "democracy," and "capitalism." Neo-Jacobin ideology should be further differentiated by comparing and contrasting it with more traditional notions of man, society, and the world. More light can be thrown on the new Jacobinism by indicating what it is not and by suggesting alternatives to its beliefs.

The above analysis has found "equality" and resentment of traditional elites to be a central neo-Jacobin preoccupation. As the new Jacobins are convinced of their own intellectual superiority and are rather condescending towards the common people except in official ideological and ceremonial contexts, their passion for equality may be at bottom a desire to remove obstacles to their own ascent to power.

The work of Allan Bloom, one of the most widely read and celebrated contributors to neo-Jacobin ideology, is here as in other respects particularly instructive. One of the most striking features of his *The Closing of the American Mind* is its deep prejudice against traditional communities and social hierarchies and particularly the conventions and attitudes of aristocratic and upper-class society. The very principle of the aristocratic appears tainted.

Bloom finds social contract theory very appealing. The reason is that it places all human beings on par. A premise of social contract

155

theory is that society is not man's natural condition but owes its existence to a contract made between equal individuals in a pre-social state of nature. In that condition, man's real nature was most fully revealed. All were free to act as they pleased. Historically existing societies, in contrast, may violate the basic needs of human nature. Rousseau saw a sharp contrast between the natural state and the present, social state of man. According to him, man in the state of nature was good, free, and happy. All were equal. The now-existing civilized society has enslaved man and destroyed equality. It has built up elaborate structures and expectations that imprison man's goodness. Elites, most especially the aristocracy, are the very embodiment of artificiality and perversion of nature. They have no legitimate claim to authority, are in fact evil conspirators against the good of the people. Another social contract theorist whom Bloom likes is John Locke. He, too, assumed that in the state of nature men were free and equal. They entered civil society only to remedy certain "inconveniences" of the state of nature relating to the insecurity of property. Locke's depiction of the pre-civil state contained an implicit attack on existing traditional elites and property arrangements. He suggested that only labor and skill entitle a person to property, and he emphasized utilitarian, entrepreneurial effort, as distinguished from spiritual, contemplative and artistic pursuits, as signs of being a real person: "God gave the world . . . to the use of the industrious and the rational (and *labour* was to be *his title* to it:)"[2] Locke's *Second Treatise* implied the need for a rather drastic revision of the existing social and political pecking order, promoting the self-made man and demoting people born to social prominence or not engaged in utilitarian work.

Rousseau and Locke can be, and frequently have been, sharply criticized. It has been pointed out that the notion of a state of nature is artificial, that it is based not on historical investigation but on pure speculation. In all of known history man has lived in society, and, for all of the imperfections of society, it is there that he has achieved such wellbeing as he enjoys. Social contract theorists attribute to man in a pre-social condition traits that could have developed only in society. Their view of man reveals a lack of understanding of what human strengths and abilities owe to his being born into society and his being the beneficiary of the effort of previous generations. Social contract theory lacks the historical sense. It is abstract and philosophically strained.

But social contract theory appeals to Bloom, because it treats all human beings as equals. It deflates traditional elites: "It pulls the magic carpet out from under the feet of kings and nobles." According to Bloom, John Locke has been unfairly criticized for superficiality by defenders of traditional society. The reason for their not liking him, Bloom explains, is that "he was not a snob." It is fashionable to deny, Bloom observes, that there ever was a state of nature. He adds, "We are like aristocrats who do not care to know that our ancestors were once savages."[3]

Locke and Rousseau and the third major social contract theorist, Thomas Hobbes, are for Bloom not above criticism, especially not Hobbes, but they were of groundbreaking importance, he believes, in that their assumption of human equality made possible a new beginning in theory—just as the discovery of the new world promised a new beginning in practice.

Again and again, the emphasis on equality and the desire for a fresh start establishes a strong link between the old and the new Jacobins. The French Revolution is for Bloom clearly a force for good. He does not hide his dislike for those Europeans who tried to stem the revolutionary tide, those to whom he refers as "the right." The right, he contends, has but one "serious meaning": it is "the party opposed to equality." Bloom has little or no sympathy for defenders of the old order in Europe or America. These conservatives may have feared the disappearance of the noble and the sacred and a general narrowing and vulgarization of life, but Bloom rejects these sentiments as "the special pleading of the reactionaries." He sharply criticizes the American South for not accepting what he asserts to be "the heart" of the U.S. Constitution, its "moral commitment to equality." The opposition in the South to "mass society," "money grubbing," "technology," and the destruction of organic and rooted community appealed only to reactionary "malcontents."[4] What must be taken much more seriously, Bloom contends, are the ideas of the French Revolution. More generally, he rejects the charge that the Enlightenment has an overly optimistic view of human nature and society. This reputation has been created by self-serving reactionaries.

Given the centrality of equality in new and old Jacobin ideology, some special attention should be given to how it contrasts with another possible view of society and elites, one that can be described as more or less continuous with the older Western understanding of human existence. Such a comparison will help demonstrate the scope of what the new Jacobinism rejects while indicating an alternative to its way of thinking. More needs to be said here and in the chapters to follow about how Western society might begin to move out of its precarious state rather than letting the new Jacobinism aggravate that situation. This chapter will show that a Jacobin advocacy of equality is a major source of the problems of Western democracy.

Attempts by traditional conservatives to blame the decline of Western society in the twentieth century on a "revolt of the masses" were largely misdirected. These conservatives absolved those who must bear the brunt of any blame: the Western elites. The catering to popular tastes today and the advance of plebiscitary democracy is not the result of relentless pressure from the grass roots but of elites proclaiming the wisdom of "the people" or their moral right to rule, mobilizing the masses and granting them preferment. This empowerment gives power to—new elites. All societies are class societies of one type or another. Some of the most markedly and inflexibly stratified class societies were created in the name of equality, the Soviet Union with its *nomenklatura* being a prominent example. What can vary greatly is the form of the class system, which can be elastic or rigid, humane or inhumane.

Among those who set the tone in America today—in the arts and entertainment, the media, the universities, politics, and business—the moral, cultural, and intellectual assumptions associated with the old Western civilization have not been dominant for a long time. Many in these elites are systematically attacking what remains of those assumptions. They not only condone but also generate the growing nastiness, crassness, vulgarity, debauchery, and mediocrity of life. From corporate boardrooms to lecture halls, courtrooms to movie studios, foundation boards to pulpits, legislatures to newsrooms, traditional civilization is gasping for air. Many within the American elites do resist the general trends, some bravely and with limited success, but they do not think of themselves as being on the winning side. Many tell themselves that the situation is not as bad as it seems.

Some try, rather pathetically, to imagine themselves members of the ruling class by riding horses on their country estate, lunching at the Metropolitan Club, or attending Sunday services with nice people at the Episcopal Church.

The slow but sure abdication of the old American elites, due in large part to their having become converts themselves to the need for rejecting old-fashioned conduct and thinking, serves the neo-Jacobin desire to replace the old elites with themselves. The neo-Jacobin defense of universal principles and opposition to the more extreme manifestations of social and cultural disintegration makes them seem a stabilizing, conservative force. The impression is deceptive. One reasons is the notion of equality that the new Jacobins embrace. That notion is a powerful acid eroding the already crumbling foundations of the old Western society.

Americans have always been deeply ambivalent about social class. Many have resented traditional Western elites, associating them with injustice and oppression. Thomas Jefferson declared it a "folly" to think that "kings, nobles and priests" would serve the public good. On the contrary, they form a "confederacy against the happiness of the mass of the people."[5] Populist impulses and social resentment have competed in America with a desire for elites. Though Jefferson wished for a "natural aristocracy," he was a committed populist and majoritarian. But for a long time the plebiscitary impulse was kept under control for the most part by American leaders and intellectuals of a different cast of mind, including the Framers of the U.S. Constitution. That document forbids titles of nobility, but American society soon evolved a leadership class not dissimilar to that of old England. Today many Americans have an almost fawning attitude towards European royalty and nobility. Some Americans still play at being British gentry, as witness the horse farms and mansions found on the outskirts of America's great cities and elsewhere. Significantly, as has been shown, the original U.S. Constitution set up quasi-aristocratic institutions. Unable to bestow titles of nobility, American presidents instead hand out Medals of Freedom and other awards.

All elites are prone to self-centeredness, arbitrariness, conceit, and inbreeding. The remedy, the new Jacobins and many others contend, is "equal opportunity." This principle will, it is asserted, give merit what it deserves. America, so it said, has found a way of rewarding ability without creating a class society. But a classless society is an illusion, and talk of "equality of opportunity" overlooks that civilization is defined by its way of discriminating among and ranking abilities. Men being prone to what is easy rather than what is difficult and admirable, civilization does not leave discernment of high and low to the majority, just as it does not leave it to "market forces." It creates structures for promoting and protecting the highest human aspirations.

Civilization lives by its discriminations and rankings. It penalizes some human inclinations and rewards others. Gatekeepers of many kinds and at many levels push some individuals forward and hold others back. Civilization favors the wise and virtuous, not the superficial and dissolute, honors responsible statesmen, courageous soldiers, good students, excellent artists, honest businessmen and careful craftsmen, not opportunists, cowards, slackers, pornographers, shysters, and fakers, however able. As discussed briefly above, it is of the very essence of civilization *not* to give equal opportunity.

A proponent of "equality of opportunity" might object that all he opposes is *arbitrary* or *illegitimate* denial of opportunity, but that objection begs the all-important question of how properly to discriminate. It is through *un*equal opportunity that society encourages individuals to give their best and discourages the opposite. Besides, "equality" is in the end a pure abstraction, a mathematical idea, which is impossible to convert into social reality.

A classical, "well-rounded" education used to be considered basic for people destined for influence. The Greek discipline of *paideia* formed the whole person. It was intended to prepare the individual for the life of the good, the true, and the beautiful by fostering physical vigor, intellectual and aesthetical discernment, and, above all, moral character. Members of influential elites had to be first of all civilized, broad-minded human beings, whatever their special functions in society. In combination with good social background and experience, sound education was thought to produce the gentleman, the person qualified for gatekeeping.

Many champions of "equality of opportunity" would have all doors flung wide open to merit. Why should a bright, knowledgeable lawyer not advance quickly in the law firm and in general society? Perhaps he should, but hardly if he is also a blatant self-promoter, an amoral hired gun, and a person who knows or cares little about the connection of the law to the higher purposes of society. A surgeon highly skilled at wielding his instruments might also be checked at the gate and found socially wanting for having a truncated, cynical view of life and choosing his specialty according to profitability—characteristics that are only seemingly irrelevant to dealing properly with human beings and practicing medicine. Civilization will always have and may even need some condescension and snobbishness.

It used to be said that it takes three generations for family wealth to produce aristocratic breadth and refinement, but there are of course exceptions. Individuals of humble social origins sometimes contribute greatly to civilization. Burke still may have had a point: "The road to eminence and power, from obscure condition, ought not to be made too easy, nor a thing too much of course. If rare merit be the rarest of all rare things, it ought to pass through some sort of probation. The temple of honor ought to be seated on an eminence." Employing a lax or narrow definition of merit may facilitate social circulation, but only circulation of a certain type. Advancement will be made easier, but only for some, and soon the resulting inferior elites will impose their own criteria for how people can measure up. These may be even narrower and less stringent. Eventually truly humane and civilized persons will start to appear odd and out of place in their society and be denied the influence that they deserve. Burke's comment on the era inaugurated by the French Revolution is here relevant: "The age of chivalry is gone. That of sophisters, economists, and calculators has succeeded; and the glory of Europe is extinguished forever."[6] Burke was too uncritical of the old order, partly for rhetorical purposes, but he also did not know the worst of what was to come.

A society would be fortunate whose most truly admirable individuals set the standards for the rest. That they be in a position to do so is a central, though always unattainable, purpose of civilization. Sound elites will exhibit flexibility and tolerance in granting admission to their circle, but, to ensure the tethering of expertise and ability to the humane purposes of life, they will look for more than utilitarian "skill" and sheer energy in those whom they promote.

Many distinguish between "equality of results," which is supposed to be bad, and "equality at the starting line," which is supposed to be good. So routinely are formulas of this kind used, that they are sometimes repeated even by highly intelligent persons. Paul Johnson, for example, writes, "The end result cannot be equality, but from start to finish the rules must apply equally to all."[7] Just as Johnson is no egalitarian, so is he not a utilitarian, and he probably is unaware of the full ramifications of his statement. Formulas of this type about equality of opportunity are reductionist and conceal complex reality. What is overlooked is that every society is the product of long development. There can be no such thing as a starting line where "equals" start seizing their opportunities. Historically evolved civilized and civilizing social structures and preferences by their very nature create inequality of opportunity. Equality at the starting line would presuppose emptying society of whatever makes it civilized. As already mentioned, all could not start from scratch without abolishing inheritance.

Was it perhaps a desire for equality of opportunity that until not long ago gave the United States the most confiscatory estate taxes in the Western world? Or were those taxes inspired by the related presumption that self-made men are the most admirable and the only ones really entitled to their property? This consideration brings up the deep American prejudice in favor of people engaged in utilitarian as distinguished from contemplative and artistic pursuits. This prejudice is sometimes so pronounced and one-sided that success in business is assumed automatically to qualify a person for influence in other areas and—if the success is sufficiently great—for the presidency.

The old Western tradition had a very different bias. The narrow and mercenary attitudes assumed to be characteristic of people in trade and production made them less than suitable for inclusion in the highest social and political circles, which required breadth of mind and sensibility. This bias reflected the classical Greek ideal that those should set the tone who were capable of partnership in the life of the good, the true, and the beautiful. Property is merely an indispensable means to this end. The active life of *leisure*, not busyness, was the highest form of life, a notion that helped define the Western idea of the gentleman. Members of the Western "bourgeoisie" modeled themselves on the non-utilitarian attitudes of the aristocracy, which is one of the ways in which the higher purposes of life were integrated into economic life.

Especially in America, disparagement of non-utilitarian pursuits has long militated against the highest form of gatekeeping. The trend can be traced back in the English-speaking world to John Locke, among others. His latitudinarian version of Puritan Christianity helped elevate the self-made, "productive" man by asserting that it is by "mixing his labor" with things in nature that value is created and a person becomes entitled to ownership. Busily working away at tangibly useful tasks is pleasing to God. Locke's emphasis demoted "non-productive," contemplative work and corresponding elites. He counseled that the young be educated for a life of usefulness and gain. Much that had been highly valued in earlier Western culture Locke disparaged, as when he wrote that "parents should labour to have [the poetic vein] stifled and suppressed" in their children. Poetry usually goes together with gaming, he asserted, and they are alike in that they "seldom bring any Advantage."[8]

One of the preconditions for the formation of new, discriminating American elites would be the rediscovery of the centrality of non-utilitarian endeavor. A floundering, disoriented civilization can hardly be rescued by uncultured makers and doers. Unfortunately, doers of a nasty kind are often the ones to take advantage of desperate circumstances. In the long run, only a broad reinvigoration of Western society—of mind, imagination, and moral character—can reverse existing trends. What specific elites would emerge from such a development cannot be foretold. All that can be predicted is that they would put hucksters, smut-peddlers, demagogues, and other blatant self-seekers in their place.

The new Jacobins offer their ideology as giving America and the West a needed sense of direction and mission. But their conception of equality is very hard to reconcile with maintaining civilization, at least of a traditional kind; indeed that conception will serve to remove whatever remains of the older standards of conduct and the corresponding type of elite. Jacobin equality will help clear away social, political, intellectual, and cultural obstacles to the reign of Jacobinism. The virtue with which the new Jacobins would like to replace the old Western ways may be able to create an order of sorts, but it will be an order imposed from above rather than an order emerging from within individuals striving to civilize and humanize themselves.

Notes

1. Jaffa, "Equality as a Conservative Principle," 88.
2. John Locke, *Second Treatise of Civil Government* (Indianapolis, IN: Hackett Publishing Co., 1980), §34, 21 (emphasis in original).
3. Bloom, *Closing,* 162, 293.
4. Ibid., 159, 32.
5. Jefferson, *Life and Selected Writings*, 394-95.
6. Burke, *Reflections*, 44, 66.
7. Paul Johnson, "The Moral Dilemma Confronting Capitalism," *Washington Times*, February 21, 1989.
8. John Locke, *Second Treatise* and *Some Thoughts Concerning Education* in *The Educational Writings of John Locke*, ed. James Axtell (Cambridge: Cambridge University Press, 1968), §174, 284.

16

A Center that Cannot Hold

"In America your destiny is not prescribed; it is constructed. Your life is like a blank sheet of paper and you are the artist."—Dinesh D'Souza[1]

"By recognizing and accepting man's natural rights, men found a fundamental basis of unity and sameness . . . . [N]atural rights . . . give men common interests and make them truly brothers"—Allan Bloom[2]

The new Jacobins believe that social unity derives in its most important aspect from an ideological like-mindedness among virtuous citizens. The various traditional, religious, and other cultural traits that may have shaped a people are, from the point of view of political morality, secondary or dispensable, and may even be obstacles to the kind of cohesion that stems from a common devotion to principle. In this perspective, America is an "idea," a country founded on universal principles, rather than a historically formed nation intimately connected to the old traditions of Western civilization.

Because the New Jacobins do not see historically evolved order as a morally significant source of unity, they favor placing few restrictions on immigration into the United States (and other Western countries). That new arrivals often have cultural backgrounds much different from American tradition matters little, because to be an American is primarily to believe in "American principles." These are universal and can be rather quickly imparted to immigrants. Indeed, most of the latter are, so it is said, drawn to the United States precisely because of its principles.

Although this chapter will deal with the problem of immigration with special reference to American circumstances, the general issues involved are equally relevant to Europe, with adjustments for cultural differences. Neo-Jacobin thinking on immigration into the United

States corresponds to very similar thinking across the Atlantic about immigration into the countries of Europe.

There is plentiful historical evidence that cultural diversity and immigration need not undermine a society's cohesion. They can be sources of cultural enrichment and renewal. Especially in a strong, vibrant society or civilization, groups of different religious, ethnic, and national origin may be pulled, however reluctantly in particular cases, into a dynamic and fertile consensus. With regard to individual immigrants, who could dispute that the United States has benefited greatly from persons of special ability from virtually every ethnic and racial group having come to America?

It is possible to be in favor of generous rules of immigration and to be worried nevertheless about the sheer size and the cultural composition of legal and illegal immigration into the United States in recent decades. Not only is legal immigration at a historical peak; illegal immigration is rampant. A 2002 study commissioned by the U.S. Immigration and Naturalization Service concluded that, because of inadequate screening methods and limited resources, between 2.95 and 5.45 million illegal aliens enter the United States *each year* through the nation's ports of entry by using bogus documents. Another 3 to 5 million illegal aliens enter through unguarded areas.[3] Someone alert to the depth and breadth of America's social problems and aware of what social and political order owes to the like-mindedness produced by a common history cannot fail but be concerned about issues of social unity and cultural and political continuity.

For many years, an attempt was made in the United States to match immigration to the cultural origins of the earlier Americans. It was thought that such a policy would facilitate assimilation and help maintain the cultural and political identity of the United States, including its tradition of constitutionalism and liberty, which is a product of Anglo-Saxon and European civilization. Through 1970, Europeans made up more than half of the immigrants. In 2000, they represented only 15.8 percent. Latinos made up 51.7 percent and Asians 26.4 percent. From 1990 to 2000, the foreign-born population of the United States grew from 7.9 percent to 11.1 percent, which is the fastest growth rate in the last 150 years.[4] The number of foreign-born residents is higher than at any time in American history. Half of the residents of New York City are legal or illegal immigrants.[5] In

Miami, 75 percent of the population speaks a language other than English at home, and 40 percent of that city's population is foreign-born. In Los Angeles, 31 percent of the population is foreign-born. At the same time, many new Americans and resident aliens resist integration into American culture; some groups cultivate separate ethnic or racial identities. As president of Mexico, Vincente Fox encouraged Mexicans who emigrate to the United States to consider themselves still Mexicans and to vote in the interest of their native country in American elections.

An article in the *Washington Post* in 2002 gave the following snapshot of the new multicultural America:

> This week, some 3,000 ethnic media representatives from 500 newspapers, magazines, TV and radio stations and online publications will gather at the Hilton in Beverly Hills . . . . It's an event that has been largely ignored . . . despite the seismic shifts the gathering represents in a state that's often recognized as the harbinger of things to come . . . . Seven major ethnic dailies in the state, 30 Vietnamese publications in Orange County, 15 Thai-language newspapers in Los Angeles, several 24-hour radio stations for Pashto and Dari speakers, and 14 Filipino media outlets in the San Francisco Bay area are just a few of the voices making up our remarkable *Tower of Bable* . . . . If you can't understand what your fellow subway rider is reading, if you can't follow the opinions he or she listens to each night, how can you hope to hold a discussion about national or even neighborhood politics?[6]

The nature and scope of the social change brought by immigration is a big and complex subject, but there is no disputing that, especially in some parts of the United States, large-scale immigration is having a major impact on mores, language patterns, and political attitudes. The change is obvious even to the most casual observer. In many places, traditional America is barely recognizable. The extent and speed of the transformation of America is suggested by the following data. In the ten years between the 1990 and 2000 census, the six New England States together with New York, New Jersey, and Pennsylvania lost 2.7 million residents, who moved to other parts of the country. The figure is equivalent to the population of Connecticut. This loss of population was more than made up by the entry of 3.1 million immigrants, which the *Washington Post* calls "the largest surge of immigrants since the first decade of the twentieth century."[7]

The impact of mass immigration and what can be called cultural separatism cannot be assessed without considering the ever-present need to balance unity and diversity. It is important to ask whether American culture still has sufficient centripetal and harmonizing pull to avert social fragmentation. Whatever other problems may be caused by multiculturalism and immigration, today they are straining an increasingly fragile social fabric. The question arises whether there are sufficient sources of order in American society, actual or potential, to moderate and balance the centrifugal influences. Or does the strain on society need to be reduced? The same questions are relevant to European circumstances.

The neo-Jacobins sharply criticize the ideology of multiculturalism. They see the affirmation by particular groups of distinct cultural identities as undermining the virtuous unity that comes from embracing the American "idea." Still, the new Jacobins regard large-scale immigration favorably. They trust in American principles to unify the United States.

Yet most Americans seem to sense a growing social and political fragmentation and a general loss of unity. They also appear to have difficulty identifying the central cause of that unease. Though in the present historical circumstances immigration and separatism may be putting a great strain on the United States, a strong case can be made that the fragmenting of society comes, in its most important dimension, from disintegration at the moral core of civilization. American society faces large-scale legal and illegal immigration and multiculturalism at a time when, as previously discussed, the traditional ethic of character and personal responsibility is losing its strength and prestige.

To reiterate and extend an earlier argument, the old moral ethos stressed personal obligations to individuals up close. This virtue made possible a society that was, at the same time, decentralized and morally cohesive. The cohesion derived from recognition of a universal moral authority above contending interests and from citizens working to harmonize their lives accordingly. They were not unified mainly by doctrinal agreement. Neither were they unified by national boosterism. Tension was reduced through acts of self-discipline, fellow-feeling, and kindness. Social harmony was understood to require good character and conduct first of all. There were no short cuts to a better society. A larger social good, including the preservation of freedom, was seen as dependent on imperfect and sinful human beings restraining their lower desires and trying to develop their higher natures. The importance of local and central government was recognized, as was the need for religious, moral, intellectual, and cultural authority, but the primary responsibility for dealing with problems was understood to rest with those most immediately concerned.

From this understanding of virtue and social life grew a highly decentralized, group-oriented society. The common good was not considered the same as conforming to an ideological plan—which is the notion of unity held by the French Jacobins and their descendants today. Diversity did not have to be abolished. The common good was seen as entailing respect for and adjustment to the legitimate needs and interests of individuals, groups, localities, and regions. Diversity would be made compatible with diversity through self-restraint and consideration for others—again, not in theory merely but in concrete, actual conduct.

The virtue of moral self-discipline and effort is being replaced today by the ever more brazen self-gratification of individuals and groups. People who shy away from the rigors of the old virtue of character but who still would like to think of themselves as moral have available to them new conceptions of virtue, of which the Jacobin one is prominent. These conceptions are appealing in that they do not demand any difficult improvement of self. They make it possible to qualify as virtuous either by emoting benevolence or by keeping the right ideas in one's head. As in the case of the French Jacobins, the two modes of morality often blend in one and the same person. The more sentimental of the two is altruistic sympathy, tearful compassion for favored suffering groups. The more rationalistic virtue centers on ideological profession of "justice," "rights," "equality," or "democracy." What they have in common is an evasion of the need to shape character. This means that they neglect what may be the most basic requirement of civilized life.

The problem of order and freedom was summed up by Edmund Burke as follows: "Men are qualified for civil liberty in exact proportion to their disposition to put moral chains upon their own appetites . . . . Society cannot exist unless a controlling power upon will and appetite be placed somewhere, and the less of it there is within, the more there must be without."[8] Lack of self-discipline among society's members increases the need for externally imposed controls. The present is clearly a time of weakening internal checks. To the strain on social order is now added cultural separatism and large-scale immigration, legal and illegal. The conclusion seems inescapable: Social cohesion will increasingly have to be imposed from without.

The present situation in the United States regarding immigration and multicultural pressures was anticipated with typical prescience and precision over three quarters of a century ago by Irving Babbitt. In 1924, he wrote in characteristic style, "We are assured . . . that the highly heterogeneous elements that enter into our population will, like various instruments in an orchestra, merely result in a richer harmony; they will, one may reply, provided that, like an orchestra, they be properly led. Otherwise the outcome may be an unexampled cacophony."⁹

Babbitt's analysis of the moral circumstances of the modern world bears directly on the prerequisites of order in a culturally more diverse America. He addressed the needs of an era in which Christianity would retreat as a disciplining and harmonizing influence and in which a shrinking world would create growing interaction between different populations. He formulated the central problem as follows: "The special danger of the present time is an increasing material contact between national and racial groups that remain spiritually alien."¹⁰ These circumstances require special moral, intellectual, and cultural effort, including identification and cultivation of the ecumenical element in the higher religions and ethical traditions. The needs of this era could not be met by sentimental and abstract universalism. The latter would, on the contrary, worsen a problematic situation. Babbitt was unmistakably and unabashedly American, but he was also a cosmopolitan. He called for respecting and seeking the common ground with other cultures. The problem of tensions between peoples could not be solved by trying to efface existing identities.

The very different neo-Jacobin view of how to achieve social and political unity is that the consensus of civilization, with its roots in the moral and cultural striving of generations of individuals, can and should be replaced with ideological unity based on reason. Order is supposed to result when all are taught to accept the same allegedly universal ideas. According to this view—which may be called the civics approach to social order—not even open borders need present

any serious problem, provided that the new arrivals are properly in-
structed, which is supposedly facilitated by their being already prone
to embracing the same universal principles.

The civics approach associates what it calls virtue with adherence
to the right ideas. It fails to recognize the nature of moral character
and how important it is to social and political order. It also underes-
timates the extent to which moral and other order evolve historically.
The civics approach assumes that social and political unity can and
should be derived from proper ahistorical thinking and instruction at
whatever time and place it is needed. In reality, a more than superficial sense of common purpose emerges only from the protracted
effort and cooperation of many generations, as a sense of universality adapts to and expresses itself in the actual, concrete circumstances
of a people. Genuine as opposed to imposed and artificial social and
political order owes immeasurably to cultural continuity, to the ab-
sorption and cultivation, in practice as well as theory, of the best of a
historical heritage. A past that continues to live in the present helps
inspire and direct new human effort. The slow initiation into civilized life across a broad range of human concerns is something very
different from learning to mouth certain formulas said to contain
universal principles.

The failure to understand society as a historically created and evolving human community marked the thinking of John Locke. For him,
order and freedom are made possible by the rationality of the individuals who live at a particular time. Even before the establishment
of civil society, individuals had the capacity, through reason, to live
free and ordered lives. This condition comes naturally to man. "We
are born free as we are born rational," Locke wrote.[11] Freedom is not
the result of long struggle by human beings who strive within a society to govern themselves and remove obstacles to liberty and who in
time create the circumstances in which freedom becomes possible.
Freedom does not emerge out of such historical struggle. It was for
Locke, as it is for the new Jacobins, a free gift of nature. Locke had
little awareness of the degree to which freedom and peaceful conditions presuppose strength of character and other civilized disposi-
tions in individuals and of how much these traits owe to the effort of
earlier generations, which have been transmitted through living traditions. According to Locke, order and freedom have their source in

abstract rationality. He did not recognize that the ability to reason does itself evolve historically and socially and that reason is very far from being some purely individual faculty. Locke simply placed rationality and other civilized traits among the natural attributes of an imaginary pre-social, autonomous, and independent individual. The particular human self, as it exists outside of every cultural context, was assumed by Locke to have the resources necessary for an ordered existence. The self is not defined by any particular cultural identity. Lockean individuals belong nowhere and everywhere. In their morally significant aspect, they are abstract, ahistorical beings. They are socially interchangeable. Under this view, which is very appealing to the new Jacobins, it matters little to social unity what social and historical origin individuals may have. The new Jacobins assert on the basis of such thinking that ideas acquired in the abstract can substitute for that slowly and laboriously acquired civilized personality and society that, according to Edmund Burke, is, by far, the most important source of liberty and social cohesion.

An ahistorical view of society akin to that of Locke is reflected in the notion, cherished by the new Jacobins, that the United States is a young country, a fresh start for humanity. That view appeals greatly to persons who want to leave the old Western civilization behind. But except in the sense that America was settled in new geographic territory, the United States is no younger than any other Western country. Its roots are deep in the distant European past and beyond. That Americans do not have on their territory ancient buildings and monuments to remind them of the age of their civilization makes it easier to maintain the myth of America's youthfulness, but there is more to a society than what meets the superficial and ideologically willful eye. As has already been discussed, the Framers of the Constitution and the American people at large were imbued with classical and Christian prejudices and habits, which helped shape the work at Philadelphia. From the point of view of what ensured America's social and political order, the least significant part of the Constitution was the written document. Far more important was the unwritten constitution, all of the religious, moral, intellectual, and aesthetical habits and attitudes that are implied in the written Constitution. Without them the document would not have been conceived as it was, and without them it could not have been successfully put into practice.

From the beginning, a Lockean or quasi-Lockean view of the nature of man and society had adherents in America, as it did in other parts of the English-speaking world. Thomas Jefferson is a prominent example of one who took Locke very seriously. But a more historically grounded conception of the United States as having its origins in a British and European past was clearly the predominant one. To the extent that the latter understanding drew upon Locke, it associated Lockean "rights" with the historically concrete Rights of Englishmen and in general fitted Locke into the wider Western civilization out of which America had come. In time, intellectuals began attributing more and more significance to the Lockean dimension of America. This suited those who were uncomfortable with the conservative implications of America's actual origins and who wanted to move America in a much different direction. In the twentieth century it became routine to refer to the United States and the Constitution as the product of Lockean thinking. The work of disconnecting America from a past that was deemed unpalatable was facilitated by also defining Locke as a secular modern liberal. A new myth of America was created, the America of a fresh start, of abstract rights and principles and of enlightened secularism. This marked change in the self-understanding of Americans contributed greatly to the deepening divisions within the country. The United States became increasingly schizophrenic, a country pointed in one direction by its historical origins and in a very different direction by the evolution of its intellectual and cultural life. To this schizophrenic condition, which relates to larger trends and tensions within Western civilization as a whole, has been added the problem of massive immigration.

Previous chapters have established that the new Jacobins like to think of the United States as resulting from a "Founding." They like the sound of that word because it conjures up the image that the country was made up more or less from scratch by individuals with excellent ideas. "Lawgivers" bestowed a plan on a supposedly bewildered American people and gave Americans a common identity and purpose. As has been shown, for Allan Bloom the central meaning of the United States is the implementation of a rational plan for "freedom and equality." "This is a regime founded by philosophers and their students," writes Bloom. "America is actually nothing but a great stage" on which theories have been acted out. "There are almost no accidents."[12]

American unity was thus spun out of a few enlightened minds. Abstract ideas, not historically formed personalities, built the United States. We have seen that, in Bloom's interpretation, the Framers were on much the same wavelength as Rousseau and the French revolutionaries. The Framers had a plan for an egalitarian and majoritarian order that the American people adopted, being rescued, presumably, from earlier disorder and confusion.

It was the intent of the Framers, Bloom insists, to phase out cultural particularity. In his view, historical identities threaten ideological unity and should give way to like-mindedness. The Framers did not desire a harmony of different legitimate interests but ideological homogeneity. What is admirable about America, according to the new Jacobins, is separate from its uniqueness as a historically shaped nation. America is held together and "ennobled" by universal principles. These exist apart from, and even in conflict with, old cultural traditions and identities. The new Jacobins claim to defend the "principles of Western civilization," but their defense is highly selective. They are suspicious of, even hostile to, the older Western civilization. The civics approach, or the "Great Books" approach influenced by the same kind of thinking, becomes instruction towards preconceived ideological conclusions—indoctrination rather than education. In as much as this kind of education neglects just how the older Western heritage nurtures personal character and responsibility, the social cohesion to which it aspires must be supplied in practice by ideological intimidation and, finally, by police and courts of law.

It would seem highly relevant to the issue of immigration that the United States is an extension of European and English civilization. The Constitution that the Framers wrote was indistinguishable from the unwritten constitution, including the virtue of character at the heart of traditional Western civilization. Although that ethos overlaps in some respects with non-Western civilizations, America's political institutions and its corresponding traditions connect the United States primarily with Europe, especially England. The long-term effect of large-scale immigration from societies that have been largely untouched by traditional Western civilization in general and by the Anglo-Saxon political tradition in particular is unclear. It is possible that immigrants from East Asia, say, will bring cultural traits to the American pool that will shore up habits of self-discipline or that bring about desirable cross-fertilization, but the present troubles of American society, and of European society, can hardly be overcome by trying to import moral and other forms of culture. A resurgence of American civilization of the needed depth and scope must surely spring from within the historically rooted American national character itself and from the larger civilization to which it belongs. In the absence of that kind of revival, large-scale immigration into the United States is likely to worsen drastically the problem of fragmentation and further undermine American constitutionalism and liberty.

Though only a resurgence of Western and American culture can buttress American social and political order, it should be reiterated that sound patriotism always has an ingredient of cosmopolitan and aristocratic breadth. The needed creative and unifying spark cannot be supplied by populist nationalism, which pins its hopes for national renewal on an idealized common man or "middle class." For all his possible strengths, the common man is at least as prone to the weaknesses of human nature as others, and he has a good deal less knowledge, intelligence, imagination, and breadth of understanding than many members of elites. Unfortunately, the illusion survives that the common people are a repository of virtue and wisdom. The democratism examined in this book feeds that illusion, even as it promotes the reign of yet another elite.

Whatever the tactical, short-range benefits of an opportunistic populism in trying to rein in or dislodge present dubious elites, it has little to contribute towards a cultural revitalization. A renewal of American and Western civilization, assuming that one is still possible, would require advanced ethical, intellectual, aesthetical, and political creativity and leadership. New elites would have to form and replace or sway the present ones. What could be more superficial than the idea that a couple of electoral triumphs for "the people" might set America right?

It can be plausibly argued that there are few signs of America's dominant elites sobering up or being edged out by leaders of a different kind. Continued neglect or mishandling of acute social problems may in time produce more explosive fragmentation and tension. The day could come, even in the United States, when power-seeking demagogues focus the resulting popular resentment on immigrants and outsiders and propose drastic measures to "save" society. Should that day come, all bets are off. To avert that prospect would require realistic, circumspect, and courageous leadership. In their neglect of the moral and cultural crux of America's problems and in their simultaneous encouragement of large-scale immigration, the new Jacobins exacerbate a difficult and even ominous situation.

Notes

1. Dinesh D'Souza, *What's So Great About America* (Washington, DC: Regnery, 2002).
2. Bloom, Closing, 27.
3. Study commissioned by the U.S. Immigration and Naturalization Service, 2002, as reported in the *Washington Times*, December 5, 2002.
4. Figures from the 2000 U.S. census, *Washington Times*, June 5, 2002.
5. Report by the Northeastern University Center for Labor Market Studies, 2002.
6. Margaret Engel, *Washington Post*, September 15, 2002.
7. *Washington Post*, July 22, 2002.
8. Edmund Burke, *A Letter to a Member of the National Assembly in Answer to Some Objections to His Book on French Affairs*, 1791.
9. Babbitt, *Democracy*, 271.
10. Irving Babbitt, *On Being Creative* (New York: Biblo and Tannen, 1968; first published by Houghton Mifflin in 1932), 235.
11. Locke, *Second Treatise*, 61, 34.
12. Bloom, *Closing,* 97.

17

Responsible Nationhood

"It will be the century of an interconnected transnational world. It is a world in which inhuman ideas are collapsing of their own rottenness, and shared humanizing ideas will have a chance to flourish."—Max Lerner[1]

"Everyone believes in freedom and equality and the rights consequent to them."
—Allan Bloom[2]

The desire of the new Jacobins to spread "democracy" has been illustrated and analyzed with considerable care. Though they present this desire as an expression of benevolence and caring for peoples not yet enjoying self-rule, the will to power behind their democratism is blatant and importunate. A particular country will have to take charge of the task to improve the world, the one that is based on universal principles. Particular individuals, the ones who understand those principles the best, should lead this great effort or, at minimum, advise the decision-makers. Whether the power that the new Jacobins seek is to be enjoyed personally and in political practice or merely vicariously, their wish to tell other countries how to behave is palpable.

Neo-Jacobins like to cite the formula that democracies are never warlike, but sometimes democracies are precisely that. In 1914, for instance, all male electorates in Europe greeted what would become the First World War with great enthusiasm. The Jacobin faith is itself militant. Its claims are by definition universalistic, and it implies the moral perversity of forms of rule and social organization that do not conform to its democratist prescriptions. The new Jacobins are disinclined to tolerate disagreement and are inclined to assertiveness and aggression even without some obvious provocation to their own country.

The events of September 11 were a heinous provocation. These atrocities and the debate about whether to go to war with Iraq and other countries provided a strong stimulus for the neo-Jacobin impulse and also a perfect opportunity for neo-Jacobin agitation. The new Jacobins could take advantage of the rightful indignation of Americans to spread their notion that they represent virtue and are called to defeat evil in the world. The new Jacobins were among the first to call for military action not just against the perpetrators of these deeds of terrorism but against states and other entities posing any kind of threat, present or potential, to the United States or its friends. The great complexity of the issues involved, including the long-term consequences for America and the Western world of large-scale war, would not restrain their moralistic belligerence. To dwell on such issues seemed to the new Jacobins morally evasive. What was needed was "moral clarity." The implication was obvious: they were arguing the case of moral right, whereas those not accepting their views were morally obtuse or perverse. In their claim to know better than all others and to be paragons of political virtue the new Jacobins again showed themselves the descendants of Rousseau and the old Jacobins. Those figures of the past also believed that life offers clear-cut moral choices, even in the world of politics. They, too, ignored the fact that political reality is always highly intricate and to some extent contradictory, often obscure and confusing and full of shades of gray rather than sharp contrasts of black and white. Jacobins, old and new, simply assume that they can discern clearly what is good and evil. Good is what they like, and evil is what their opponents like. Gone is the old Greek and Christian prejudice against pride, and gone is the old view, most emphatically stated by Augustine, that *all* human motives and *all* political causes are suspect.

The new Jacobins never needed exceptional events or acute threats to the United States to push their agenda for changing the world. Their mind-set is intrinsically expansionist. The new Jacobins would, of course, deny that their desire to remake particular countries has anything to do with a hunger for power. Their interest is solely to fight evil and promote the good of the particular people and the rest of the world. What affected states may regard as bullying or belligerence is, from the point of view of the new Jacobins, but moral indignation against wrong and righteousness in a noble cause. Babbitt wrote, "A democracy, the realistic observer is forced to conclude, is likely to be idealistic in its feelings about itself, but imperialistic in its practice."[3] What is neo-Jacobin moralism and ideology if not a sanction for imperialism?

A monopolistic ideological universalism that scorns historically formed societies is a potential source of unending war and great disasters. Yet to warn about this mind-set and subject it to philosophical criticism is not the same as to denigrate universality in every sense. One possible consequence of dismissing every notion of universality would be to encourage those who stress national particularity as the defining attribute of political and cultural life. Nationalists resist the idea that there might be some bond connecting human beings from different societies, to say nothing of human beings from different civilizations. Such a bond might put limits on national self-assertion. It could provide an appeal for the weak against the strong. Nationalism is prone to self-absorption and therefore to disdain for others and to bellicosity. Paradoxical though it may seem at first blush, unbounded nationalism has a great deal in common with abstract universalism. Both reject checks on their will to dominate. As we have seen, that will is strong among the new Jacobins. The blending of democratism with the desire to turn the United States into a great missionary power dissolves the line between nationalism and universalistic ideology. The resulting nationalistic democratism hides yet other motives.

Both nationalism and abstract universalism clash fundamentally with recognition of the conception of universality that has been described here as compatible with the decentralized and group-oriented society in general and with American constitutionalism in particular. Understanding the basic moral issues involved is equally important to thinking about international affairs. It is crucial to be aware of the sharply different meanings and implications of the two forms of universalism. The current state of public debate on U.S. foreign policy and international politics is, in this respect, woefully inadequate. Not only is current discussion making do with broad, philosophically crude generalities. When it comes to ethics it also assumes that a certain kind of ideological universalism—democratism—is the only possible moral basis of foreign policy. As the terms of this debate directly affect the behavior of the most powerful nation in the world, the situation is dangerous. One of the aims of this book has been to introduce into public discussion an alternative to neo-Jacobin universalism. The analysis that follows will extend earlier arguments in order to show that the moral issue of foreign affairs can be addressed without either resorting to ideological moralism or denying the relevance of morality.

The proposed understanding of universality, here as related to international relations, is as far removed from a sentimental belief in the brotherhood of man as it is from so-called "realism," the approach to foreign affairs that simply dispenses with moral considerations. Though the very first requirement of political morality must surely be to have no illusions about what can be expected in politics, cynicism is a fake realism and an abdication of moral responsibility. Genuine morality is fully compatible with taking politics as it really is. Morality will explore fruitful political opportunities even in discouraging circumstances. At a time of international tension it is possible to try, without naiveté but also without moral pretentiousness, to discern what might be best for all the countries involved. Real political morality does not try to impose *the* right solution, which, given the diversity and complexity of the world, is a fiction. Political morality makes its contribution rather by identifying and countering obvious ruthlessness and unmitigated arrogance and by encouraging sensitivity to the legitimate concerns of all relevant parties.

It has been shown that Jean-Jacques Rousseau is simultaneously the intellectual father of Jacobinism, the French Revolution, and nationalism. What he calls the general will unifies a particular people only. There is no moral authority beyond it with reference to which conflicts among peoples might be mitigated. Individuals should derive their moral identity exclusively from the general will, and loyalty to "the fatherland" must inspire all their actions. This collective national identity must supplant every other membership and be the sole source of personhood.[4]

In attributing the general will to a particular people within a fairly small society Rousseau's notion of political morality retained a limited, if strained, connection with the old Western society of regions and local communities. But not only does Rousseau insist that virtue has nothing whatever to do with a differentiated, decentralized, group-oriented society of the traditional kind; his moral and political philosophy also assumes that the world has to be remade according to his newly discovered view of man and society. Significantly, his universalistic claims were soon and very easily detached by his followers from his anachronistic and romantic attachment to the size and purported unity of the city-state of Sparta or a Swiss canton. The French Jacobins quickly adapted Rousseau's thinking to much larger political ambitions, and the Jacobins of our era, aware of the potentialities opened up by modern communication and technology, not least of a military kind, have literally globalist aspirations, giving the will to power a hitherto unimaginable scope.

The idea that lay implicit in Rousseau's thought—that the new virtue must sweep the world and form a single collective whole—has become central to the new Jacobinism. Max Lerner gave the idea explicit expression in 1988: American freedoms, he asserted, "are the freedoms for which the outside world yearns." Optimistically and benevolently, he speculated that the peoples around the world would finally have their wish before the end of the twentieth century. Lerner hoped that humanity could "look forward to a global social contract between nations and their leaders," to a worldwide "moral community."[5]

This vision of the world transformed could hardly be better suited to an unlimited and uncompromising will to power. Given the gloriousness of the goal, who could be permitted to resist? Why should such good intentions tolerate evil? Presumably, peoples and leaders wishing to remain outside of the proposed global social contract would have to be forced to be free, to repeat Rousseau's phrase for how to deal with those who are not in tune with the virtuous general will.

The neo-Jacobin view of the world splits humanity into two camps, those wishing the good of humanity and those perversely resisting it. Here as in so many other ways the new Jacobins follow Rousseau, for whom political opinions are either moral or immoral: the line between good and evil is not blurry; good and evil are not found on all sides. For Karl Marx, social and political existence was defined not by moral community or nationality but by class, but Marx, too, split humanity into separate camps that could not hope to co-exist or accommodate each other. His notion of the inevitable, unrelieved, and intensifying conflict between the bourgeoisie and the proletariat denied the existence of a common humanity that would make it possible for human beings to see beyond their different economic interests and through which they might come to recognize the legitimacy of claims other than their own. Marx denied, in effect, that people of different backgrounds might resonate to, and be humanized by, the same poetry, art, music, or moral example. Had Marx admitted the possibility of a shared human frame of reference that operated right across the disagreements and diversity of human beings, he would have had to accept the possibility of a muting of hostilities, of a give-and-take between interests, even of reconciliation among them.

The new Jacobinism resembles Marxism in that it does not contemplate compromise or mutual respect between those who are doing mankind's bidding and those who stand in their way. Universal principles must prevail. You are either for or against political virtue, which is to say that conflict will always be in the air.

The criticism that can be directed against Rousseau, Marx, or the new Jacobins on this score applies to any social and political analysis that treats a single particular attribute or membership—individuality, class, tribe, state, nationality, ideology—as salient, distinct, definitive, and self-sufficient: life becomes a struggle of "me" or "us" against "them." Persons or political entities must, in the end, confront each other as belligerents. Whether of an economistic, nationalistic, biologistic, or ideological cast, this kind of view of man and society employs philosophically artificial categories. It simply ignores the infinite intricacy of human existence and the deeper affinities among human beings. It extracts an artificially and reductionistically constructed element from highly complex living reality and decrees it to be fundamental to understanding life and defining politics. Whether this view rejects or accepts universality in some form, it flatly denies that universality might be organically, synthetically related to particularity, that historically evolved societies and personalities might offer different embodiments of the same quality of higher life.

This last-mentioned possibility should be explicitly related to international relations. Although a particular human being is and remains unique, personhood develops within family, other associations, country and a more broadly encompassing civilization. The last permeates all the others, and the life of individuals and of a broad range of sub-divisions shape the civilization. But each of these memberships, if they are not of some strangely warped, primitive, confining, self-obsessed type, point beyond themselves. True community and civilization carry the person beyond personal idiosyncrasies, tribe, region, and, as important, the particular time in history. It is in the nature of civilization to discriminate against whatever threatens its central values, but it is never merely self-enclosed. Its sense of the good, the true, and the beautiful connects it, however tenuously in some cases, with mankind at large. The great exemplars of morality, thought, and art speak, at least potentially, to all of humanity, however difficult it may be for particular individuals and peoples to absorb their achievements. In times of acute domestic or international strife, passion may dim the awareness of a universal humanity in the minds of the most intense partisans, so that they pursue the foe with unrestrained intolerance and viciousness. In the case of more civilized persons, not even violent conflict will obliterate the recognition that a common humanity hides behind the warring interests of the moment and that today's enemy may and should be tomorrow's friend. This thought is not negated by the fact that political and other actors sometimes behave so abominably, in peace or war, that they separate themselves from the rest of humanity and cannot return.

The pursuit of genuine universality is not a matter of different individuals, countries, and civilizations stripping themselves bare of historically inherited traits and embracing the tenets of an ideology, as the new Jacobins assert. A particular tradition is made distinctive by the needs and opportunities of historical circumstance, but it is also, to the extent that it embodies the deeper concerns shared by all human beings, a window on other similarly motivated traditions. As has been pointed out before with regard to the patriotic love of a particular country, sound tradition always has a cosmopolitan dimension. By virtue of the element of universality in his own background, the civilized member of a particular society can to some extent recognize people who live in what may seem a much different cultural setting. He may be acutely sensitive to the deficiencies of other societies and still discover in them manifestations of the same civilized striving that he knows from his own culture. This can be the case even if the family resemblance is faint, undeveloped, or distorted. An important task of the civilized person who takes an interest in international affairs or in particular countries is to look for opportunities to broaden and deepen the sphere of a common higher humanity—which is something very different from imposing preconceived ideological nostrums on those who are different. The imagination and learning of the cosmopolitan give him the ability to empathize and identify with his counterparts in other countries. They make him subtle and flexible and prepare him to discern opportunities for mutual cultural enrichment. These opportunities can be humbling in that they may undermine assumptions of automatic superiority in particular fields.

It bears repeating that the same higher values can be pursued and realized differently depending on time and place. The civilized person may be especially fond of the tradition he knows best, partly because it is the tradition that he has had the chance to penetrate the most deeply and that has most directly shaped his upbringing, but he delights in the diversity and richness of human life and in what other societies can contribute to his own and to the whole of humanity.

The mutual dependence of universality and particularity is as significant within as among societies. The intent of the American Framers, for example, has been shown not to be the obliteration of diversity. They hoped for a harmonization of many interests. From this kind of unification the whole society could draw strength. What would hold the nation together, besides sturdily constructed political institutions, was the self-limitation and mutual respect of different regions, communities, groups, and interests—a condition made possible not merely by enlightened self-interest but by recognizing a higher humanity that both transcends and embraces diversity.

Jacobin moral and political unity, domestic or international, is centrally generated moral homogeneity achieved at the expense of diversity. Like nationalism of the bad kind, Jacobinism produces an artficial, boosterish togetherness that is inherently condescending to everything but itself.

To nationalists who identify only with their own people and stress what separates them from the rest of humanity, the term "cosmopolitan" has the distasteful connotations of cultural rootlessness and lack of loyalty to a particular country. By a "cosmopolitan" they mean someone who is culturally, if not geographically, homeless in the world and who has no deep affection for his own society as a historically formed nation. Individuals who actually fit that description in their personal lives may be relatively uncommon, but, in theory at least, the new Jacobins do think of themselves as being ideologically above national culture and national divisions. They are "citizens of the world." They represent a great cause rather than a culturally distinctive country. On these grounds the new Jacobins may regard themselves and be regarded by others as "cosmopolitans," but under the definition offered here it would be inappropriate so to classify them— because of their rather provincial notion of what is good for all peoples, because of their rigid adherence to their own principles, and because of their disinterest in or hostility to traditional societies. As has been suggested before, the real cosmopolitan is not self-absorbed but alert to and welcoming of the possible strengths of other nations. He is open to the possibility that his own tastes and beliefs are not what they should be. That real cosmopolitans are rooted in and attached to the best of their own heritage may lead Jacobin universalists to call them "nationalists," "nativists," "isolationists" or the like, but these terms do in some respects apply a good deal better to the new Jacobins themselves, given their contempt for other points of view, their self-satisfied moralism, narrowly political focus, and preoccupation with their own ideology.

Those who treat class, nation, or other entities as ultimates and who view conflict as the essential truth about politics like to think of themselves as realists who see through the illusions of "idealists": They are cutting through moralistic verbiage and getting down to the power realities that are the essence of politics. Granted, Machiavelli and Hobbes do offer important lessons about the requirements of political order. Their perspectives are relevant to a world that remains full of conflict and not least to the Western democracies which are showing growing signs of fragmentation. Yet a political philosophy is deficient that does not fully recognize the existence and political significance of what transcends conflict. A reductionist stress on politics as pure partisanship reveals a constricted view of politics. A preoccupation of this kind is less than hard nosed, because it does not fully understand the meaning and sources of power. The entire human personality participates in politics, and human motives are not reducible to a single drive or function. Moral conscience, too, can have an appreciable effect, even though it must usually find its way in situations dominated by very different motives. It is commonly assumed that morality is ill adapted to the realities of politics, that it is faint and ethereal and has no chance of making a difference outside of the more peaceful circumstances of private life. Widely circulating idealistic notions of morality may have contributed to the wrongheaded dismissal of morality as irrelevant to actual political life, as distinguished from the imaginary politics of idealistic theory. But it is possible to regard morality quite differently. It can be seen as a force that does not flee from but stands up to the pressures of politics. By being practical, adaptive, inventive, and assertive it can advance its own interests in the world as it is.

What "realist" students of politics also tend to disregard is the decisive influence wielded by individuals who might appear not to be involved in practical politics at all, but who nevertheless are highly influential in setting the stage for what is politically possible. They are the persons who, because of their roles in the arts, universities, entertainment, and communication, can capture the mind and the imagination of a people and shape their sensibilities, hopes and fears, their way of seeing reality. Whoever has access to the inner life of a people can affect the wellsprings of action and make particular policies seem palatable or unpalatable.[6]

Heavy-handed assertions of an artificial national or other particularity can accomplish no real or lasting renewal of national character. A reinvigoration and development of the national heritage along the lines of what was earlier called responsible nationhood would indeed involve the cultivation and further development of a historical national identity, but not in a manner to pit "us" against "them." A properly restored sense of national identity would, in a sense, strengthen the bond with mankind at large, for it would be inspired by a love of one's own that transcends fondness for the particular. One's own would be cherished as a culturally distinctive manifestation of a common humanity. Responsible nationhood is fully compatible with pride and assertiveness in defense of important and legitimate interests, but in its underlying peaceful demeanor it is conducive to respect for and harmonious relations with other countries.

A renewed quest for the universal, then, must not be confused with a desire to impose abstract, ideological constructs or with a corresponding pursuit of unlimited power. In a time like ours, especially, when the moral center appears to be barely holding, the universal must be sought first and foremost in the strengthening and deepening of the life of individuals in the families and communities where they spend most of their lives. It has been suggested in this book that, though universality has different dimensions—moral, intellectual, and cultural—which are in a sense equally important, the civilized society depends first and foremost on personal character. Individual moral responsibility creates and maintains the foundation for a society that treasures the true and the beautiful along with the ethical. The latter is, over time especially, the most basic requirement for a life worth living.

What today's Western society seems to need most is the rediscovery of responsibilities that are near, immediate, and concrete. Contrary to democratist rhetoric, America and the Western world may be best served by heeding the ancient moral tradition that makes it the primary obligation of individuals, communities, or countries to try to make the best of their own lives and to remedy their own most glaring flaws. There is never any shortage of such work to be done, and today the task is so extensive and urgent that it will require great concentration and energy. To set out instead to try to remake the world according to an ideological blueprint represents not only moral arrogance but a flight from responsibilities at home that are large and pressing. The United States is in some important respects dramatically better off than many countries, but that fact does not make its own problems any less acute or menacing or give it a mandate to dictate how other countries should live. A will to power that is so ambitious as to portray itself as benevolence for all mankind is always dangerous, but in the morally, intellectually, and aesthetically depleted and disoriented Western world of today the resistance to utopian appeals has been greatly weakened. The neo-Jacobin calls upon the United States to take charge of the world may have disastrous consequences, internationally and domestically. Many Americans, Europeans, and others who become uneasy at the mention of a New World Order react that way partly because they fear that to a great extent this order will be defined and constructed not by individuals of cosmopolitan sophistication and discernment but by power-seeking utopian ideologues.

A great power like the United States has far-reaching interests and great international responsibilities. Like all nations, it derives indispensable benefits from contact with other nations. Yet in the current situation, in which so many neglect grave domestic problems and consider plans for global reconstruction, Americans and others might do well to listen to John Randolph of Roanoke (1773-1833), the prominent congressman and orator. Randolph was ever alert to threats to liberty coming from inattention to near responsibilities, centralized power, and expansionist ambition. He feared the effects of a decline of American character on American freedom. In opposing federally funded and directed road and canal projects to encourage westward expansion, projects touted at the time as "internal improvements," Randolph, in 1826, penned a critique that can be read also as a counterweight to the impulse to have American power encompass the world:

> We do stand in need of "internal improvement"—beginning in our own bosoms, extending to our families and plantations, or whatever our occupation might be; and the man that stays at home and minds his own business, is the man that is doing all that can be done (rebus existentibus) to mitigate the evils of the times.[7]

It is neither possible nor desirable for the United States simply to "stay at home." But the evidence presented in this book indicates that a major influence on U.S. foreign policy, neo-Jacobin democratism, is based on highly dubious and inflammatory ideological assumptions and on a voracious appetite for power. The new Jacobinism is a recipe for perpetual conflict. It would seem that, beyond the need to resist globalist ambition, U.S. foreign policy should be bounded by urgent and basic needs at home and by the self-restraint and realism of cosmopolitan patriotism. The present, we keep hearing, is, because of the crumbling of communism, an era of great political and economic opportunity. The neo-Jacobin desire for international intervention and adventurism on a large scale shows that it is also an era of great peril.

Notes

1.   Max Lerner, *Washington Times*, May 17, 1990.
2.   Bloom, *Closing*, 162.
3.   Babbitt, *Democracy*, 293-4.
4.   Rousseau, *Poland*, 19, and *Social Contract*, esp. bk. II, ch. 7.
5.   Max Lerner, *Washington Times*, January 2, 1988.
6.   On the "non-political" sources of power, see Claes G. Ryn, "Dimensions of Power," *Humanitas*, Vol. XIII, No. 2 (2000).
7.   John Randolph to John Brockenbrough, August 10, 1826 (Hugh Garland, *The Life of John Randolph of Roanoke*, New York, 1850, II, 309).

18

Needed: A New Moral Realism

"As long as the United States of America is determined and strong this will . . . be an age of liberty, here and across the world."—George W. Bush[1]

"America is no mere international citizen. It is the dominant power in the world, more dominant than any since Rome. Accordingly, America is in a position to reshape norms, alter expectations and create new realities. How? By unapologetic and implacable demonstrations of will."—Charles Krauthammer[2]

"America, with its vast power, can sometimes seem like a bully on the world stage. But, really, the 1,200-pound gorilla is an underachiever in the bullying business."—Robert Kagan[3]

At the end of the Cold War, Americans who had been strong advocates of military and other firmness against the Soviet Union broke into two camps. The one assumed that it would now be appropriate to reduce the country's vast military and other international commitments. These had been due to extraordinary circumstances. Given the broad interests of the United States, there would be no question of radically disarming or of withdrawing behind the borders of the country, but neither would there be any need for an extensive military presence in Europe and more distant places. The second camp was made up of those "hawks" whose reflexes from the Cold War were not appreciably affected by the changed international situation. They were accustomed to and attracted to the use of American power, and they saw new reasons why the United States should maintain its heavy involvement in international affairs and retain its military strength. Idealistic-sounding neo-Jacobin rhetoric about spreading democracy and other good things to the rest of the world helped justify their ambitions and was especially appealing as it had antecedents in modern American history. There could be no better excuse for exercising American power than creating a better world for mankind. That goal created virtually unlimited opportunities for expanding the reach of the United States. Already during the Cold War, many of these hawks had been neo-Jacobins. They had been ardent opponents of the Soviet Union not merely because they saw a need to resist and defeat a dangerous enemy, but because they wanted their own vision for the world to be implemented. Now that the Soviet empire had collapsed, they saw an opening for expanding their own.

Though many neo-Jacobins knew quite well what they wanted, it would be an exaggeration to say that neo-Jacobin ideology as a whole was deliberately and consciously constructed as a justification for empire. Yet whatever motives inspired the shaping of this ideology, its conception of universal principles and of a new world provided a strong impetus for pushing outward. At the bottom of neo-Jacobinism is an unwillingness to tolerate any society that does not conform to its own ideological preferences. To want to rid the world of unacceptable societies and keep it clean is by definition an imperialistic ambition.

As if serving neo-Jacobin aspirations, the United States is not significantly reducing its commitments and limiting its objectives. One example will suffice. The North Atlantic Treaty Organization came into being to defend Europe and the West against a large and acute threat, but after the disappearance of that threat NATO has been *expanded*, and there are plans, though complicated by tensions over the war in Iraq, for making it even bigger. American commitments are growing correspondingly. Many European governments prefer to spend their resources on social programs rather than defense and have let the United States provide for some of their military needs. The United States is happily doing so, in considerable part because of neo-Jacobin advocacy. Europe can hardly be left to its own devices. Whether intended or not, the plans to preserve and extend NATO lets the United States preserve and extend its control over Europe and adjoining areas. But if these particular developments leave some room for speculation about American motives, the comprehensive strategic plans embraced not just by neo-Jacobin theorists but by people in charge of American foreign and security policy leave no doubt about the imperialistic ambitions of leading Americans.

Neo-Jacobinism is the main factor behind the quest for American world supremacy; hence the need for understanding it thoroughly. It is troubling to recall the bloodshed and enormous suffering to which Jacobin power seeking and moral and intellectual arrogance have exposed mankind. An extreme manifestation of the Jacobin spirit, Marxism, is no longer a politically potent force, but another scheme for transforming the world has replaced it. The new vision of humanity redeemed may strike many people in the Western world as appealing and as very different from Marxism, but, as this book has shown, neo-Jacobin universalism is by no means unrelated to the earlier form of universalism.

The new Jacobins have worked to expand their influence within a democratic society whose laws and norms of appropriate behavior, though increasingly shaky, still impose some limits on political action. The new Jacobins have not yet exhibited the kind of political ruthlessness that was characteristic of Marxism and French Jacobinism before it. Yet their diligent and cliquish pursuit of power and their ideological fervor are reminiscent of those of the Marxists and the old Jacobins. There are grounds for suspecting that, upon gaining a firmer hold on power, the new Jacobins will gravitate in the direction of more despotic methods. They are already employing systematic demonization and ostracism of their critics and the attempted destruction not only of their reputations but also of their livelihood. As the restraints of American constitutionalism continue to deteriorate, military or other emergencies will provide neo-Jacobin leaders widening opportunities for silencing their opponents as well as for imposing general restrictions on civil liberties. The neo-Jacobin movement already exercises great influence in the United States, especially within the foreign policy establishment, and it has potentially unobstructed access to great military power, the CIA, the FBI, and the Department of Homeland Security.

Though philosophically not particularly sophisticated, neo-Jacobin ideology is sufficiently coherent and comprehensive to attract people of intelligence and to serve the mentioned objectives well. It enjoys at least limited academic credibility outside of its own school and affiliated groups. It is very well represented in departments of political science in American universities, especially in the sub-fields of political theory, national security, international relations, and American national government. A large number of students with under-graduate or advanced degrees who are imprinted more or less with the neo-Jacobin mind-set move each year into the wider society. Many take positions as staffers in such places as the U.S. Congress, the White House, the departments of the federal government, think tanks, magazines, journals, newspapers, radio and television, and, of course, academia itself. The new Jacobinism has a very large network of intellectuals and political activists, which virtually ensures that its leading figures, however modest their accomplishments, will enjoy high reputations and respectful treatment. Neo-Jacobinism is highly visible in the major media. Its commentators are ubiquitous on television, in leading newspapers, and on the radio. Those who join the neo-Jacobin network can expect to derive substantial benefits from their membership, just as those who spurn or oppose it can expect the opposite.

Neo-Jacobin advocacy of abstract, globalistic ideas and of a concomitant expansion and concentration of political power is today common in both of the major American political parties. The political and other differences between Democrats and Republicans who are attracted to this point of view are fairly insignificant compared to what they have in common. Though many of the ideologically most intense and aggressive neo-Jacobins are found in the Republican Party and are called conservatives or neoconservatives, the same general outlook is well represented in the Democratic Party and among people called liberals. The *New York Times* columnist Thomas L. Friedman speaks for many of them. Describing the leadership needed in America and the world, Friedman writes, "The Administration, from whichever party is in power, is going to have to bring together the new globalizers . . . to form a new twenty-first-century coalition that can defend free trade and American internationalism."[4] A person of leftist background who advocates American imperialism is Paul Berman, author of *Terror and Liberalism*. Berman believes that the United States must lead the progressive forces in the world against the enemies of freedom, especially Islamic fundamentalism, which he considers a dangerous "fascist" threat.[5] The neo-Jacobin impulse is shared by many neoconservatives, liberals, and leftists who make common cause in pushing for American global ascendancy.

The new Jacobins have thought and acted strategically and have very successfully promoted their political and intellectual agenda.

One of the reasons is that their ideology corresponds to or serves powerful business and financial interests. These define themselves in opposition to traditional cultures and state sovereignties and oppose all obstacles to trade and investment. The new Jacobins are far advanced in achieving their goal of directing the future of America and the West. Their ideology provides the moral-intellectual justification for continuing to depose traditional elites and installing a new ruling class.

Of those who advance the neo-Jacobin cause far from all are committed and self-conscious promoters of its ideas. Some assist it by merely parroting its themes, a practice known to help careers and increase income. Often neo-Jacobin objectives are unwittingly assisted by individuals who simply do not understand what those objectives are. Some politicians uncritically adopt the language of more deliberate advisors and speechwriters. Many exhibit the neo-Jacobin mind-set in diluted or partial form. Sometimes neo-Jacobin ideas acquire credibility by becoming loosely associated with respectable intellectual positions that may be superficially similar in some respects but are ultimately quite different. Many who think of themselves as Western traditionalists carelessly mix neo-Jacobin elements of thought with ideas of their own that are only tangentially compatible. One example—somewhat pathetic because it shows the vulnerability of traditionalists who have difficulty finding a philosophical footing in the modern world—are rationalistic neo-Thomist Christians who think that neo-Jacobin advocacy of "natural right" and "universal principles" must surely be much the same thing as a defense of "natural law." Some Christians of this type may be prone to neo-Jacobin thinking in the first place, but a lack of philosophical maturity and learning also makes it easier to hold divergent ideas together. A particularly striking example of intellectual bewilderment and helplessness are intellectuals who think of themselves as conservatives but who are unthinkingly embracing much of the heritage of the French Revolution. Another example are putative conservatives who assume that a conservative is someone who is more inclined than others to use military power or bullying against other countries.

To sort out what is what and to establish the contrast between the new Jacobinism and the more traditional moral, cultural, and philosophical beliefs and practices that made constitutional democracy possible has been a central purpose of this book. A failure to make appropriate distinctions is a dangerous feature of today's public debate. Key terms have to be dichotomized. That so much of the discussion of democracy ignores or glosses over distinctions of fundamental importance is a source of major intellectual and practical confusion and has direct and major political consequences.

To an extraordinary extent, American intellectuals who claim to be defenders of Western civilization and the American Constitution are at loggerheads with themselves, pulling in different directions at the same time. They are simply unaware, or manage to conceal from themselves, that they are embracing discordant elements of thought and morality. Many neoconservatives are in this predicament. They mix sound and unsound, constructive and destructive ideas in sometimes odd combinations. It is partly because of this widespread and insidious confusion that this book has sought to lay bare the moral-intellectual dynamic of neo-Jacobinism and explain what it really is. One might hope that persons who are made aware of the nature of the neo-Jacobin component of their own thought and imagination will begin to extract themselves from what will, in the end, prove a morally and intellectually very compromising affiliation.

Many neoconservatives have probably been held back from disassociating themselves from the neo-Jacobins by fear of losing access to the media, sources of approbation, publicity and income, and, perhaps as important as anything else, fear of having their reputations blackened. Many rather traditional conservative intellectuals, who must surely have some awareness of what they are doing, seem, for whatever reasons, to go out of their way to reassure and please neo-Jacobin arbiters of acceptable opinion.

The new Jacobins have managed through political-ideological passion and diligence, planning, organization, largesse or stinginess, smokescreens, and intimidation to discourage or neutralize dissenting opinion among those who might have been expected to challenge most vigorously their claim to being "defenders of the West." Many liberals who are not very fond of the old Western civilization but who lack the ideological stridency of the new Jacobins have also, for the most part, refrained from confronting them, despite the fact that their belligerence, particularly in foreign policy, must at times have created considerable unease.

For reasons mentioned earlier there is considerable tension between neo-Jacobin and postmodernist critics of traditional Western society. From the point of view of the former, postmodernist radicals go much too far; in attacking all inherited political, cultural, and intellectual structures they threaten also the Enlightenment and Jacobinism. Nevertheless, the new Jacobins are assisted by postmodernist radicals in that they are discrediting the ancient Western civilization and breaking down the remaining defenses of the old West. They help to destroy lingering traditional institutions and elites. Radical postmodernists constitute an essentially negative, disparate, for the most part patently extreme, often intellectually frivolous and undisciplined movement that is also not strongly prone to political organization. For that reason, the new Jacobins do not greatly fear them as competitors for political power. Also, for the new Jacobins to be able to criticize the value nihilism and recklessness of postmodernism helps maintain the appearance that the new Jacobinism is a mainstream, conservative movement standing up for America.

The inclination of the Western democracies to look away from acute problems is ominous. Current deleterious trends cannot be broken unless the patterns of reality-avoidance are broken. If Americans and other Westerners are inclined to choose ideology and wishful thinking over critical reflection and realism, not only will the Western world as previously known simply peter out, its disappearance will probably be accompanied by great social and political turbulence and anxiety.

Equally dangerous is the hostility with which those who dominate public opinion greet ideas different from their own that attempt to deal in depth with festering problems. The Western democracies are receptive to pretentious sociopolitical proposals inspired by abstract and sentimental virtue, but most of these schemes do more to aggravate than alleviate problems. Only superficially does the neo-Jacobin espousal of "moral values" address the needs of a morally deteriorating and fragmenting society. These panaceas exacerbate the flight from individual responsibility while indulging the will to power.

The new Jacobinism is investing the United States with a worldwide moral mission at a time of glaring moral and social troubles in America and the rest of the Western world. It distracts the individual from facing uncomfortable truths about self and society. The neo-

Jacobin myth of virtuous empire has a clearly utopian dimension. It signifies a slipping hold on reality. It can feed on a widespread wish in the general population to escape from a boring, routinized, empty, and unsatisfying existence. The imperialistic imagination of the neo-Jacobins appeals to many who want to be lifted out of a sense of personal insignificance. As the supporters of a great cause, one that involves lording it over the rest of the world, uninspired and disappointed persons can feel a new sense of importance. But neo-Jacobinism is at the same time, in many cases, a thoroughly cynical exploitation of Western moods of escape. Many of the leading new Jacobins are driven by intense ambition. Their professed beliefs are often little more than a rhetorical mask for what they want in the first place, are at times examples of the kind of clever deception that Leo Strauss counseled. The new Jacobins want to dominate others, and so their ideology commands the country over which they have influence to establish an empire.

Their will to power is restless and importunate. Whether in the name of "democracy" or by means of a more unadorned assertiveness, it wants its way. Joseph Schumpeter's description of the imperialism of ancient Rome can be read as an account of the current drive for American world dominance and especially of neo-Jacobin aggressiveness:

> There was no corner of the known world where some interest was not alleged to to be in danger or under actual attack. If the interests were not Roman, they were those of Rome's allies; and if Rome had no allies, then allies would be invented. When it was utterly impossible to contrive such an interest—why, then it was the national honor that had been insulted. The fight was always invested with an aura of legality. Rome was always being attacked by evil-minded neighbors, always fighting for a breathing space. The whole world was pervaded by a host of enemies, and it was manifestly Rome's duty to guard against their indubitably aggressive designs. They were enemies who only waited to fall on the Roman people.[6]

The new Jacobins present themselves as providing a moral response to the crisis of liberalism and relativism at home and to the problems of the world, but their ideology and will to power are far more likely to provoke international conflict than peace and to hasten rather than retard the already advanced deterioration of constitutional democracy. The neo-Jacobin abstract virtue of principles or rights, which bypasses the central moral need of character and inspires an arrogance of power, produces in practice a centralized and arbitrary form of government and corresponding international conduct. A salutary defense of constitutional government and responsible nationhood today would try to deflate, not fan, neo-Jacobin aspirations.

The present situation calls for uncompromising realism and frankness about the life-threatening problems of Western democracy and civilization. Some may contend that Western democracy appears beyond saving and that it is too late for remedies that require a long time: ways have to be found to hold back social and political disintegration. It needs to be said in response that, whatever the case, a reluctance on the part of leaders to let their ambition be checked by intellectual humility and moral self-control is the source of tyranny.

Very strong centralizing forces, domestic and international, are eroding personal, communal, local, and regional independence and control and transferring power to a small number of people. Gargantuan governments in modern Western countries and progressive globalization are great obstacles to political and social life on a more humane scale. In the United States, the federal system is so eroded that the states function almost as administrative units for the national government. The immense and continual growth of the federal government has put it in control of virtually every aspect of American life, though it chooses not yet to try to exercise every power potentially at its disposal. Uniform rules and standards of many different kinds are being imposed from the center. The U.S. Constitution no longer stands in the way of such expansion as the national government may suddenly deem desirable. The law in general is being set aside, though it is often done in the name of the Constitution and the law.

For the long term, the most important factor in the centralization and homogenization of life is not government but the evolution and centralization of general culture. Whoever shapes the mind and the imagination also shapes the future. Because of the profits that can be made by pandering to mass tastes, these tastes are overwhelming and suppressing more advanced culture. Entertainment, news reporting and opinion pitched to the lowest common denominator of millions of people flood society and foster a fatuous, passive personality type not averse to being ruled from afar. American dominance in the world of popular culture and media in Western society and elsewhere, as combined with American business and financial strength, draws more and more people into the ambit of a deteriorated civilization. Modern technology and communications exposes the entire world to an American culture of popular entertainment, one aspect of which is news that is so simplistic and flimsy that it assumes an audience not only deeply ignorant but half-witted. Global communication spreads the political opinions and general outlook of those who dominate the American mass media. As neo-Jacobins are well-represented in them, their ideological universalism has a global forum and is a major factor in the centralization and homogenization of the world and in extending neo-Jacobin control.

So strong and pervasive are these forces in today's world that a call for decentralization will appear quixotic. There is indeed no realistic prospect for substantially reversing the centralizing trends in the foreseeable future. Yet intellectuals and others who see despotic rule on the horizon have the responsibility of trying, even against all odds, to consider alternatives that might at some time begin to humanize life. Are there perhaps opportunities that are being overlooked for breaking present trends, if only in small ways? What seems utterly implausible in the present may at some future time suddenly be possible, and then the mind and the imagination should have done some of the groundwork necessary for recognizing and seizing new opportunities. All changes of any significance have to be prepared in this fashion.

Though it may appear too late now to effect the desirable change, defenders of freedom and limited government should be intensifying and expanding their arguments for drastic general decentralization. They should give serious consideration to the possibility that a giant country like the United States might reaffirm or newly create smaller units or regions. Some years ago George Kennan suggested that the United States should "be decentralized into something like a dozen constituent republics, absorbing not only the powers of the existing states but a considerable part of those of the present federal establishment."[7] This plan, which was of course greeted with incredulity by most, could be challenged on a number of grounds; it may, for instance, envision too much centralized power. But the point that is being made here is that Kennan's willingness to think in unconventional ways, even though it may have little immediate practical impact, answers to a pressing intellectual need in the current historical situation: to challenge the reigning paradigm for organizing societies and to formulate alternatives. It is no longer possible to return to the original U.S. Constitution, which was written for an agricultural republic of semi-independent states, but in rethinking present trends Americans may be aided by more than superficially revisiting the Framers' conception of central government. To resist the accumulation and abuse of power at the political center, to try to protect autonomy for local governments and private associations, and to argue for letting diverse regions and communities maintain their distinctiveness and pursue their needs according to their own best understanding is to attempt to stop a juggernaut, but to pursue objectives likes these is not to indulge in flights of ahistorical fancy. The wish to preserve local and regional control has deep roots in American and European history. Fear that the U.S. Constitution proposed in 1787 would not sufficiently respect that wish was the main reason it almost was not adopted. Today similar concerns are behind the resistance to a European super-state to be put on top of already massive European national governments.

The idea of subjecting millions and millions of people to elaborate central direction and administration is, in spite of all accompanying professions of benevolence, a sinister attack upon the humane society. It gives power to a few individuals who are also far away from the people affected by their decisions. In their current rhetoric, the new Jacobins may oppose some particular aspects of this expansion of government, but they eventually want to implement a single, unitary political scheme and see nothing wrong, in principle, with greater uniformity, so long as the uniformity is of the morally virtuous kind that they profess.

It is possible that a substantial reversal of present centralizing and homogenizing trends will not become possible except in the wake of some shattering domestic or international events that suddenly change the terms of debate and prompt new behavior. Outside of such exceptional circumstances, change of the needed proportions will, if indeed it is still in the realm of possibility, require several generations, during which mind and imagination are slowly attuned to different possibilities.

None of these observations are meant to deny that governments or international organizations have large and important functions that cannot be satisfactorily performed by any other authority. Some of these functions are inherently centralized or are not easily decentralized. But most of the accumulation and centralization of power in the Western democracies in the last century sprang from very dubious definitions of problems and from a comfortable but pernicious belief in long-distance solutions. Only a new willingness to confront the problems of life personally and up close could morally invigorate individual action and initiative and bolster private and local community. A reassertion of independence would also bring the handling of social and political matters closer to those who are most directly affected by them and most alert to local and private needs and opportunities. A reaffirmation of personal character, as distinguished from merely ideological or sentimental professions of concern for abstract collectives, would not only limit and decentralize government but also make it less arrogant, heavy handed, and bureaucratic.

It can be plausibly argued that it is not realistic, given the current major trends in the Western world, to expect Western society to sober up in this manner. But then it is necessary to face the prospect of constitutional democracy's final demise. That form of government cannot survive for long without the constitutional personality and all that nourishes that personality in the unwritten constitution of life. One thing is certain: what replaces constitutionalism will bear no resemblance to Rousseau's dream of popular rule. The new political order will be characterized by despotic, centralized power, even though—it goes without saying—that power will be exercised in the name of "democracy" and "the people."

Individuals who recognize the deterioration of Western civilization and the danger of neo-Jacobinism and who are also politically disposed and gifted will properly try to build political opposition to present trends, but so entrenched is the neo-Jacobin influence in the national media and other places where opinion is formed that this kind of effort will take exceptional courage, will power, and persistence. It will also have a very limited chance of success as long as there is but scant awareness in the American people as a whole of the precarious condition of Western civilization and of the pernicious and deceptive role played by the new Jacobins. The gradual transformation of the traditional American view of society and politics and of the political vocabulary itself have made the American public more and more receptive to neo-Jacobin appeals. Are not the new Jacobins advocating what every red-blooded American believes: that American values are the essence of political right, that these values should be exported to rest of the world, and that the United States should destroy its enemies?

Granted, public opinion may at some point begin to turn against the new Jacobinism for its recklessness or arrogance in advocating some policy or for having caused some major national misfortune. One can easily imagine a major American military intervention attributable to neo-Jacobin agitation and pressure that ends in disaster or unending conflict. Intensifying hostility to the United States around the world and large and acute dangers to America and the rest of the Western world may finally awaken politicians, opinion-molders, and the general public to the deleterious influence of the new Jacobins and set back their designs. But a lasting reversal of their rise to power would require a much better and more widespread understanding of who they are and what kind of role they are playing in American society and beyond. The ignorance, confusion and naiveté that marks so much public debate gives them cover. The crux of the problem with neo-Jacobinism is not particular individuals, however great their power, but the moral, cultural, and intellectual trends in the West that have made persons like them appear insightful and worthy of influence in the first place.

A narrowly political approach to the problem is wholly insufficient. The instruments of practical politics are, by themselves, too blunt and often leave no lasting marks. Thinking realistically and strategically about how elites are formed and deposed requires abandoning a preoccupation with elections and politicians as the key to the future. At the very minimum, it is necessary to broaden greatly the understanding of politics. Practical politics does not set its own direction; it is largely symptomatic of the moral, cultural, and intellectual life of society. What orients politics originates outside of government and parties. Politicians make a difference—a great deal of difference in some historical circumstances—but they do not autonomously generate the energy and direction of politics. In an important sense, they follow rather than lead. Politicians translate into particulars what the general trends of civilization have made to seem appealing. Only at the margins can politicians themselves steer those trends.

They are confined by the hopes and preferences dominant in their society. These bear the imprint of other elites, living or dead, of those who shape a people's mind, imagination and moral sensibilities.

Practical politics as commonly understood is, in a sense, merely symptomatic of how people imagine themselves and the world and the possibilities of their own lives. The individuals and institutions that laid the groundwork for the political transformation of the Western world were not themselves political in the ordinary sense. They were the individuals and institutions that gave people their sense of what would best satisfy their innermost longings and alleviate their deepest anxieties: poets, novelists, painters, philosophers, preachers, composers, film directors, scriptwriters, and many others, and the institutions that gave them a forum. Any real and enduring change of current trends would likewise have to start as a change in the general culture of the West.

Over time, those who shape the mind and the imagination have great power to influence the direction of social and political life. They can make the possibilities and pleasures of merely self-indulgent, comfortable living appear enticing. They can make traditional virtue look "puritanical," "intolerant," and ridiculous. They can make utopian schemes like the neo-Jacobin quest for virtuous empire seem plausible. They can make people who advocate such causes seem entitled to special respect and influence and make critics of those same causes look vile or foolish. But those who affect the mind and the imagination would be able to foster a much different outlook on life. They might attune the elites of the future to the potentialities of the good, the true, and the beautiful and alert a people to the moral and cultural prerequisites of constitutional popular government. Whatever the predominant set of ideas and cultural sensibilities of a people, it makes their will stir with particular hopes for the future and makes certain politicians look worthy of support. Society thus receives its general course largely from individuals not directly involved in practical politics. In American society today, tremendous power to shape the future is exercised by what might loosely be called the Hollywood-New York axis and the Boston-Berkeley axis.

To regard the ascendant *political* elites as the core of the problems of America and the West betrays an insufficient grasp of what ultimately moves human beings and decides the long-term direction of society. If, by some odd historical accident, the current political elites were suddenly to be sharply decimated in an election, other elites—those that mold the larger moral, imaginative, and intellectual patterns of society—would remain, and they would continue to fashion the desires and beliefs of the American people and to idolize politicians of the kind just removed.

Elites both define and embody a society's deepest longings and fears. By definition, they have the more or less grudging acceptance of a people, however much particular groups may resent their power. Western society could begin to change for the better only if budding new elites, imbued with the spirit of genuine civilization, were to convey a different sense of what is desirable and undesirable to the larger society. Such change presupposes major change in the universities, the churches, the arts, and entertainment. To state these preconditions for a transformation of Western society is to indicate the enormity of the task. That the goal seems unattainable in the foreseeable future may discourage dissenters from even attempting opposition. Even if the tide were suddenly to begin to turn, the needed change would require much time—time that may not be available. Yet dissenters would be wrong to withdraw because of the scope of the challenge and become mere spectators, hiding their demoralizing passivity behind a posture of pious disdain for what is happening. Dissenters need to do what they can, now, in whatever field is available to them. Nobody knows the potentialities of the present. All of a sudden circumstances may be more favorable to a change of course, and then the work already done by the dissenters will help maximize the benefits of the opportunity.

To save the day, some may attempt desperate but ultimately futile measures that do not address the fundamental problems. One such measure is to try reviving populism, not as a mere political expedient in difficult political circumstances, but as an ideology. This is the ideology that attributes wisdom and health to "the people" and perniciousness to elites. This formula was a theme in the thought of Thomas Jefferson, who was the closest that America came at that time to having a Rousseau among its leading figures. Perhaps the least salutary part of Jefferson's somewhat mixed and contradictory legacy is his populism: Elites should always be mistrusted, especially if they are kings, nobles, or priests, the common people not.

Government must be cleansed from time to time by the right-thinking, virtuous masses.

Populism seems plausible to many Americans today, because the elites of America's national media, universities, schools, and other cultural institutions are so clearly dominated by hostility to traditional American values. People in "the heartland" could perhaps be said to be superior to elites to the extent that they are clinging to sound tradition while the latter are recklessly abandoning it. Among the common people are the millions of decent and responsible individuals on whom American society depends for its continued operation. Popular culture at its best could be described as the wholesome ballast for the ship of state. In a time like the present, people in general may appear less obviously corrupt than their elites, but if the common people seem wiser, more "conservative," than elites, it is only because they are slow to catch on to the attitudes of the trendsetters, who are the more adventurous and creative elites. For a while in a deteriorating society people at the grass roots may keep up their protests against violations of inherited beliefs, but in the long run they will follow those who set the tone in society. People in general eventually absorb the attitudes of elites through schools, universities, churches, music, newspapers, and television. Tradition cannot defend itself without its own strong and sophisticated elites. Without that kind of leadership the erosion of tradition in general society will soon confuse and weaken the hold-outs.

As long as "common sense" survives at all, there could be nothing wrong with mobilizing ordinary people against misguided elites, but programmatic, ideological populism rests on a misunderstanding of how the world runs and of how societies develop. Reversing social decline is not chiefly a matter of kicking the scoundrels out, however important that is. It requires nothing less than the evolution of new elites across a broad range of concerns. It would be a mistake, especially in our disoriented era, to look to "the people" as the depository of moral and cultural purity and the source of social unity. If, as ideological populism assumes, the common man has such sound instincts, who is viewing all those television programs, movies, and videos, listening to all those songs, reading all those newspapers and novels, watching all those personally odious sportsfigures, adulating all those celebrities, paying all those college and university faculty, and electing and reelecting all those congressmen? Ideological populism is but another form of avoiding the deeper problem: Western civilization is slowly disintegrating.

Populist rhetoric may be defensible as a political expedient—as long as it hides no Rousseauistic illusions about the wisdom of the masses—but populism of that type is a sign of desperation, is, in effect, a declaration of political and cultural bankruptcy. It should be added that populism of all kinds plays with fire. It pursues a potentially stifling and artificial social unity. In respect to populism, right and left become difficult to tell apart.

Elites of one kind or another will always set the tone in society, even if they be the leaders of grass roots movements. On the basis of studies of the early socialist movements in Europe, all of them doctrinally committed to equality, Robert Michels formulated his famous "iron law of oligarchy." Attempts to create a "classless society" are bound to fail. As Edmund Burke wrote, "Those who attempt to level, never equalize. In all societies . . . some description [of citizens] must be uppermost." Levelers only pervert the social order: "They load the edifice of society by setting up in the air what the solidity of the structure requires to be on the ground."[8] Taken out of context, Burke's language might suggest a society sharply divided between rulers and ruled, but he means nothing of the kind. Not only is there a need for mutual respect and consideration between a people and its rulers, but there must and should be elites of many different kinds at many different levels. The important issue is what criteria will govern access to them or general advancement in society. There is no point, then, in discussing whether there ought or ought not to be elites. There always will be. The only question worth discussing is what should be "on the ground" and what should be "in the air" and how that selection might become flexible, circumspect, and humane.

The new Jacobins portray themselves as devoted friends of equality and democracy. They want these principles to triumph across the entire globe. But though the spread of Jacobin-style equality and democracy will help destroy historically evolved elites and social rankings and discriminations or more modern or radical echelons of which the new Jacobins do not approve, it will not rid the world of elites. On the contrary, the destruction of traditional societies and other socio-political structures standing in the way of neo-Jacobin plans will facilitate the rise of a new elite, whose power will be all the greater because it does not have to contend with any real competition. At bottom, the ideology of the new Jacobinism may be the more or less conscious intellectual justification for the uncontested rule of a new elite—that of the new Jacobins themselves.

To demonstrate the ideological content and practical import of neo-Jacobinism might seem tantamount to defusing its influence. Are not its abstract universalism and boundless political ambition sufficient to create fears about its influence? But the transformation of the Western and American mind, imagination, and moral sensibility has destroyed much of an older humility and sense of limits. Among the new Jacobins and others who like the idea of their country dominating other peoples, the will to power is breaking free even of the constraints of reality. So suffused is the journalistic and political culture of the United States with neo-Jacobin thinking—especially in the national media and the foreign policy establishment—that it seems an eminently plausible, almost self-evident, view of the world and of the role of the United States within it. To many, criticism of such an outlook will appear ornery, even perverse. How could anybody question the benevolent course for America, the West, and the world that the new Jacobins envision? Challenging as it does a powerful intellectual and political momentum, this book will invite surprise, incredulity, and, in the neo-Jacobin camp, hostility and abuse. Yet a forthright, in-depth analysis of the new Jacobinism and its implications for practical politics is essential to any realistic assessment of the condition of Western democracy and the prospects for change.

Have Americans become so imbued with utopianism and arrogance that nothing short of some great disaster will awaken a sense of humility and limits? Or are they still capable of heeding the advice of leading figures from their own past? The Federalist Papers, for instance, assume a view of man and politics quite different from the one popularized by the new Jacobins, although the latter often invoke the Framers to give credibility to their own ideas. Federalist No. 6 (Hamilton), which discusses international affairs, contains a pointed criticism of the kind of moral conceit and utopianism that is found at the heart of Jacobinism: "Have we not already seen enough of the fallacy and extravagance of those idle theories which have amused us with promises of an exemption from the imperfections, the weaknesses, and the evils incident to society in every shape." The same Federalist paper contains a sharp criticism of wishful thinking in international affairs that could be read as a summary of the argument of this book: "Is it not time to awake from the deceitful dream of a golden age and to adopt as a practical maxim for the direction of our political conduct that we, as well as the other inhabitants of the globe, are yet remote from the happy empire of perfect wisdom and perfect virtue?"[9]

The current desire for armed American world hegemony and the corresponding belief that the United States is called to root out evil in the world could not be in sharper contrast to an earlier American sense of priorities and appropriate international conduct. In 1821, John Quincy Adams pointed out that America had always "respected the independence of other nations" and "abstained from interference in the concerns of others" and that she had attended to her own affairs. This attitude seemed to Adams wise, for "wherever the standard of freedom and Independence has been or shall be unfurled, there will her heart, her benedictions and her prayers be." But, he continued, America "goes not abroad in search of monsters to destroy." If America embarked upon such a course she would "involve herself beyond the power of extrication, in all the wars of interest and intrigue, of individual avarice, envy, and ambition, which assume the colors and usurp the standard of freedom." In prophetic words, Adams added, "The fundamental maxims of her policy would insensibly change from *liberty* to *force* . . . . She might become the dictatress of the world. She would be no longer the ruler of her own spirit." Adams summed up America's achievement in these words. "[Her] glory is not *dominion*, but *liberty*."[10]

The advocates of virtuous empire are quick to point out that today the historical circumstances are very different from those of the 1800s and that now the United States must accept greater responsibility for the world. But behind this truism the new Jacobins conceal that they are abandoning old American virtues like modesty, prudence, self-restraint, and willingness to compromise. They are unleashing the will to power. For self-rule they are substituting rule over others.

To be the ruler of others but to be also unfree is a predicament against which Western moral and political philosophy has warned since the ancient Greeks. Christianity only reinforced these warnings. They stem from a recognition that human beings and societies are prone to destructive self-aggrandizement and other egotism. These traits enslave those whom they dominate while poisoning and rupturing relations among individuals and groups and destroying personal and political liberty. For a free society to be possible, human beings need to have humility and self-control. All social well-being emanates from properly ordered individual lives. This view finds strong support in the even older traditions of Asia. The Confucian understanding of the origins of sound political order is a case in point. The moral and political ethos of Confucianism is conveyed in the following sayings, which approve of "ancient" rulers who wanted to demonstrate their virtue to the rest of the world. These rulers wanted first to govern their own states well:

Wanting to govern well their states, they first harmonized their own clans.

Wanting to harmonize their own clan, they first cultivated themselves.

Wanting to cultivate themselves, they first corrected their minds.

Wanting to correct their minds, they first made their wills sincere.. . . .

When the will is sincere, the mind is correct.

When the mind is correct, the self is cultivated.

When the self is cultivated, the clan is harmonized.

When the clan is harmonized, the country is well governed.

When the country is well governed, there will be peace throughout the land.[11]

The ideology of American empire is derived from a very different sense of priorities and therefore from a very different notion of political virtue.

It was made clear early in this book that work towards a revival of the spirit of civilization must not take the form of an attempted imitation or repetition of the Western past. Traditionalism of a romantically nostalgic or unimaginative and rigid kind is but another example of escape from what may be an overwhelmingly difficult and therefore deeply discouraging situation. It is tempting to seek refuge from troubling times in religious and cultural withdrawal, to give up what seems a losing struggle against "the world" and to seek comfort in feelings of spiritual superiority. Traditionalism of this type is unable to come to terms with modernity in general and the existing condition of the West in particular. It is ill equipped to seize actually available opportunities for reinvigorating or shoring up civilization.

The old Western civilization cannot return. It has been too badly damaged. But the spirit of civilization can be kept alive and perhaps revived. Though always in danger of being overwhelmed by other forces, it answers to a profound human need. People in the West today who feel that need acutely will in articulating their intuitions of a better life necessarily seek guidance and inspiration in the great works of the Western past. Though perhaps unaware of it, their personalities have been shaped by a very long history, which precedes their birth; it is the history of the society that has formed them. In that society some of its most ancient ideas and behaviors have not yet been wholly obliterated, however faded they are and however ignorant those living at the moment are of their origins. Those seeking sustenance for a reawakening spirit of civilization will therefore be better able to understand and identify with the great works of their own history than the works of some other culture, though no person seeking such sustenance will in the modern global world confine himself to the study of his own past. But the main point that should be made is that, should the spirit of civilization start to undo present destructive trends, the result will not be a revival of "Western civilization." The latter is, in the end, a reification, a fetish. Only in a special and limited sense can there be a return to traditional Western civilization. It is possible to bring the Western past to bear, selectively and imaginatively, on the needs of the present. A resurgent spirit of civilization will undoubtedly make creative use of parts of the Western tradition for its new purposes, but adapting old ways and insights to new circumstances will, because of the drastic transformation of the West in the last two centuries, in effect be the building of a new society.

Any attempt to revivify the spirit of civilization must recognize that the modern world has brought major new insights and other benefits, that have to be retained and developed. Those elements of traditional Western civilization that are enduringly valid must also be restated and reconstituted in new circumstances, partly to make them understandable in a world whose moral, intellectual and aesthetical language is different from that of an earlier age. For example, as this book has demonstrated with regard to present political-intellectual discussion, some widely used terms have changed meaning. Some of them have become useless or, worse than useless, perniciously confusing or deceptive. "Western civilization" is one of them. Much is not at all what it seems.

To act intelligently one has to know and understand the obstacles and problems that have to be faced. This book was written to assist in assessing the condition of the Western world and in identifying and defining its main problems, including the threats to constitutional democratic government. It has warned in particular of the specific dangers posed by the new Jacobinism. Though most of the attention has been focused on the most powerful and trend-setting country in the Western world, this examination of the United States can be seen as a "case study" of what is happening in Western society as a whole. The phenomena analyzed here have counterparts, more or less pronounced, in all Western countries. Not only are Europeans subject to the same broad trends that have transformed American society, but they also tend to mimic American thinking and behavior.

This book has merely hinted at the general direction of efforts that might eventually check or reverse social deterioration. What is a profoundly difficult situation will require great powers of intellect and imagination and also much courage. If it is still possible to avert disaster, it may require some audacious new departures, in politics as elsewhere. The work of creative reconstruction and development needs to continue on a large scale. The stakes are enormous.

All of the arguments here presented point in the same direction: there can be no genuine and lasting recovery without a renewed awareness of personal character as the ultimate basis of the civilized society. Peace and harmony is impossible without peaceful and harmonious human beings. An exemplary society presupposes exemplary individuals. People in the Western world need to face the hard and primary obligations of the here and now, chief of which is to improve self and, in Christian language, do right by "neighbor." Efforts of this type can begin at any time. They do not have to await major positive change in society as a whole. They are themselves indispensable to such change. They can continue even in the face of further discouraging developments. Efforts of this kind, supported by a renewed dedication to learning and the arts, are the sine qua non for a revival of the spirit of civilization. Social and political life cannot be expected to serve the higher purposes of human existence unless they evolve from decent, humane individual lives. From a new moral realism might emerge a reconstituted sense of proportion and order of priorities and a more sober assessment of what can be achieved through politics.

Notes

1.   Address to joint session of Congress, September 20, 2001.
2.   Charles Krauthammer, *Time*, March 5, 2001.
3.   *Washington Post*, November 3, 2002.
4.   Thomas L. Friedman, *The Lexus and the Olive Tree*, expanded edition (New York: Anchor Books, 2000), 466.
5.   Paul Berman, *Terror and Liberalism* (New York: W. W. Norton & Co., 2003).
6.   Schumpeter, *Imperialism*, 66.
7.   George F. Kennan, *Around the Cragged Hill* (New York: Norton, 1993), 149.
8.   Burke, *Reflections*, 43.
9.   *Federalist*, 59.
10.   John Quincy Adams, Fourth of July Address, 1821, in Walter LaFeber, ed., *John Quincy Adams and American Continental Empire: Letters, Speeches & Papers* (Chicago: Quadrangle Books, 1965), 45-46.
11.   *The Great Learning* (sayings attributed to or deemed expressive of the thinking of Confucius), transl. Charles Muller, url: http://www.human.toyogakuen-u.ac.jp/ ~acmuller/contao/greatlearning.htm.

Index